Also by Jeffrey J. Fox

RAIN

WHAT A PAPERBOY LEARNED
ABOUT BUSINESS

Jeffrey J. Fox

JOSSEY-BASS
A Wiley Imprint
www.josseybass.com

Published by Jossey-Bass
A Wiley Imprint
989 Market Street, San Francisco, CA 94103-1741—www.josseybass.com

Jossey-Bass books and products are available through most bookstores. To contact Jossey-Bass directly call our Customer Care Department within the U.S. at 800-956-7739, outside the U.S. at 317-572-3986, or fax 317-572-4002.

Jossey-Bass also publishes its books in a variety of electronic formats. Some content that appears in print may not be available in electronic books.

Library of Congress Cataloging-in-Publication Data

Fox, Jeffrey J., 1945-
  Rain : what a paperboy learned about business / Jeffrey J. Fox.
    p. cm.
  ISBN 978-0-470-40853-7 (cloth)
  1. Success in business. 2. Sales management. 3. Customer relations. 4. Selling. I. Title.
  HF5386.F528 2009
  658—dc22

2008050158

Printed in the United States of America
FIRST EDITION
HB Printing   10 9 8 7 6 5 4 3 2 1

CONTENTS

Contents

EPIGRAPH

——

But February made me shiver,
With every paper I'd deliver.
DON McLEAN

If you gave me the choice of being CEO of
General Electric or IBM or General Motors, you
name it, or delivering papers, I would deliver
papers. I would. I enjoyed doing that.
WARREN BUFFETT

To Luca Modesto, Ella Elizabeth, and Dorothy Rose

PREFACE

___

Cowboys made the American West. The boys of summer made baseball the American pastime. And paperboys made the newspaper business, because if "the boys don't sell 'em, the papers don't tell 'em."

A paperboy was once the quintessential American job, symbolizing the country's relentless, indefatigable entrepreneurial spirit. There is nothing comparable. The paperboy bought, sold, delivered, and collected for the papers. And the paperboy, or papergirl, did it alone, often in the dark.

Most spectacular, paperboys were kids!

Although there are still paperboys, their ranks have been reduced for various social and economic reasons. Whatever the dynamics, there were a lot more paperboys then than there are now.

Paperboys were usually between nine and seventeen years old. Paperboys were delivering in the dark when their friends were sleeping. Paperboys were delivering in the afternoon and early evening when their friends were playing. And paperboys were delivering six or seven days a week.

Having been a paperboy is often in the bios of successful people in every walk of life. Noting that phenomenon, I have suggested in my books and talks that hiring former paperboys is smart business. In fact, after one of my talks, an accomplished, successful businessman told me, "Everything I learned about business, I learned as a paperboy." And *Rain* was born.

As the legendary Babe Ruth taught his teammates to do, I tip my cap to all the paperboys, papergirls, babysitters, lawn cutters, caddies, leaf rakers, car washers, shoe shiners, snow shovelers, and Girl Scout Cookie sellers, and to their sisters and brothers, and moms and dads.

You made America. You make America.

A *Few Famous Paperboys*

- Isaac Asimov, physicist
- Fred Bauer, Mr. Auto Wash
- Leo Bedrick, All-American athlete
- Richard Belzer, comedian
- Brandon Bergstrom, wine merchant
- Bill Bradley, professional basketball player, then U.S. senator
- Tom Brokaw, TV news anchor
- Warren Buffett, investor

- Jeffrey Burrows, entrepreneur
- Carolyn Carlstroem, publishing executive
- Sean "Diddy" Combs, singer/businessman
- Tom Chappell, founder of Tom's of Maine
- Jack Covert, founder and president, 800-CEO-READ
- Bing Crosby, singer/entertainer
- Tom Cruise, actor
- Barbara Cruz, software engineer
- Mike Daversa, CEO of Renzulli Learning
- Terrell Davis, Superbowl Most Valuable Player
- Andre Dawson, Major League Baseball player
- Walt Disney, moviemaker
- Jimmy Durante, entertainer
- Thomas Alva Edison, inventor
- Dwight D. Eisenhower, U.S. president
- Robert Frost, poet
- Stan Gault, CEO of Goodyear Tire
- Billy Gillispie, University of Kentucky basketball coach
- Wayne Gretzky, National Hockey League player
- Joe Grewe, president of Saint Gobain Glass USA
- Susan Hailey, vice president of Harrah's
- Alexander Hamilton, U.S. founding father
- Sean Hannity, political commentator

- Herb Henkel, CEO of Ingersol-Rand
- Joe Hessley, entrepreneur
- Dana Higgins, human resources manager
- Herbert Hoover, U.S. president
- Bob Hope, entertainer
- Rod Hoyng, executive vice president of Schindler USA
- Marion and Gail Hurley, mother and daughter paper delivery team
- LL Cool J, singer
- Stanley Jennings, journalist
- Bob Kelley, management consultant
- Kirk Kerkorian, investor/casinos
- Martin Luther King Jr., civil rights activist
- Gus Kontonickas, general manager of NSK
- Mitch Kotula, businessman
- Wanda Lach, dressed as a boy to hawk papers during the Great Depression
- Deborah Lacy, communications consultant
- Kelly Lane, art expert
- Ken Lewis, CEO of Bank of America
- Jack London, author
- Chris Matthews, TV journalist
- Willie Mays, Hall-of-Fame baseball player

- Don McLean, singer/songwriter
- Lynne Mica, sales consultant manager
- Allyn Miller, president of Flair Communications
- Joseph Murphy, CPA
- Terry Noonan, chief operating officer of Furon
- Bob Palka, general manager of Saint Gobain Plastics USA
- Dick Parsons, CEO of Time Warner
- Ron Paul, U.S. congressman
- Norman Vincent Peale, author of *The Power of Positive Thinking*
- H. Ross Perot, entrepreneur
- T. Boone Pickens, oilman
- Jamie Price, vice president of sales, Sandvik USA
- Sarah Rainone, book editor
- Phil Rizzuto, New York Yankee
- Jackie Robinson, first black Major League Baseball player
- Gary Rogers, CEO of Dreyer's Ice Cream
- Guy Rowland, president, Air Liquide America
- Tim Russert, *Meet the Press* anchor
- Robert "Ryno" Ryan, businessman
- Lawrence B. Ryan, businessman
- Carl Sandburg, poet
- John Schuster, creator of Superman Comics

- Jerry Seinfeld, comedian
- Gerry Sindell, author/book consultant
- Chris Skomorowski, CEO of Bicron USA
- James Stern, businessman
- Ed Sullivan, television personality
- Jeff Taylor, founder of Monster.com
- Danny Thomas, entertainer
- Dave Thomas, founder of Wendy's
- Cecil Ursprung, CEO of Reflexite
- Sam Walton, retailer
- Naomi Watts, actress
- John Wayne, actor
- Jack Welch, CEO of General Electric
- Gary White, CEO of Pacific Crest Marketing
- Todd White, National Hockey League player
- Meredith Whitney, stock analyst
- Morrill Worcester, CEO, Wreaths Across America
- Howard Wright, general manager, PPG
- Merrill Yavinsky, vice chairman of Walker-Dunlop

And there are thousands more.

Jeffrey J. Fox
Chester, Connecticut
January 2009

ACKNOWLEDGMENTS

To all the shout-outs that appear in Rain's adventures.

To Karen Murphy and Byron Schneider and the rest of the terrific Jossey-Bass team for putting a lot of life into *Rain*.

To Doris Michaels and Delia Berrigan Fakis of the DSM Literary Agency in New York City for a most professional and loyal relationship.

And to all the paperboys and papergirls and other working kids in the world.

GET UP: A PROLOGUE

R ain had been a paperboy for twenty months.
Although his bedroom was in the back of his
house, far from the street, he could hear the dreaded
sound of *The Gazette*'s delivery truck. He could hear the
truck's motor idle as it stopped at the end of his driveway. And then he heard the dreaded double thump
thump, as the delivery guy dropped two big bundles of
newspapers next to his mailbox. Thump! Thump! Get
up, chump.

Man, am I tired, thought Rain. Then the alarm
clock started. Now Rain had to get up. He deliberately
kept the alarm clock on his desk on the other side of his
room, to force him to get out of bed to shut it off. In the
summer, getting up was easier. The weather was warm.
There was a bit of daylight starting.

But it wasn't the summertime. It was February in
New England and pitch black outside. Snow piles lined
the streets, and the sidewalks were only half-shoveled.

I'd kill to stay under these warm covers, thought
Rain. But then his bare feet hit the cold floor. Alarm off.
Lights on. Rain was up. Rain was up yet again.

Rain's father said over and over: "You've got to get up to show up. If you show up, you might win. If you don't show up, you lose."

Rain hated to lose.

CHAPTER 1

OPPORTUNITY

———

I t was Saturday morning, and Mom was making
breakfast. Dad was reading the Town News section
of *The Gazette*. Rain was reading the sports pages.

"Have you noticed," Dad asked, looking up
from the paper at Rain, "that for the past few days, the
paper is finally being delivered when it's supposed to be?
In the morning?"

No one said anything.

"Would anyone like to know why the paper is
getting here on time, after weeks of late or no paper?"
Dad asked.

No one answered.

"Am I talking to myself?" Dad asked.

"Apparently," Mom said.

"Rain?" Dad said.

"What?" Rain asked, trying to read the baseball standings and look at his father at the same time.

"If you're interested and if you move fast, you might be able to get a job as a paperboy," Dad said.

Dad now had Rain's full interest. And Mom's.

"The reason the paper is being delivered on time is because a guy who works for the paper is delivering it. That kid, D.J. or P.J. or whatever his name was, who was supposed to be our paperboy, quit last week."

"Don't tell me you learned all that reading the paper," Mom said.

"No. The driver told me. He said P.J. was totally unreliable and they were probably gonna have to fire him. But he called in and quit. No notice."

"So are they looking for a new kid?" Rain asked.

"They'd probably take an adult, but, yeah, they are looking for a new kid. Here's their ad in the paper." Dad handed the paper to Rain.

Rain read the ad. Mom read the ad over Rain's shoulder.

OPPORTUNITY

Immediate opening for an ambitious person to deliver *The Gazette* in the Moravia Woods, Wellington Heights, and Lawrence Avenue neighborhoods.

Applicants must be reliable and trustworthy.

For an interview call Mr. D'Michaels.

1–800-Gazette

"Well you are certainly trustworthy and reliable," Mom said.

"Do paperboys make a lot of money?" Rain asked.

"Relatively speaking, yes," Dad replied. "For a kid your age, making twenty-five bucks a week or more is pretty good."

"Twenty-five bucks a week?" Rain repeated.

"Maybe more, maybe less. It depends on the route, how much you get per paper, and other things. But I think someone could make a lot more."

"Do you think I could get the job?" Rain asked.

"Well, first you have to want the job. Delivering papers is a tough job, and delivering the morning paper is a bear."

"How hard can it be?" Rain asked.

"Really hard," Dad said. "You've got to get up early. Fold papers. In this neighborhood, you will have to use your bike. Papers are heavy. Bad weather. But a million kids do it, and the money is good."

"I want the job," Rain said.

"Let's talk for a second. I don't want you to rush into this. You just turned thirteen, and you weigh, what, 115 pounds?" Dad asked.

And all steel, Rain boasted to himself. But he said nothing.

"A paperboy has to work seven days a week. The U.S. Post Office is the best delivery organization in the world. They deliver millions of envelopes and packages a day, but they work six days. You'll be on for seven. No break. And you'll have to spend some afternoon time to collect money from your customers."

"You won't have to spend a lot of time collecting from this customer," Mom smiled.

Dad also smiled. "I mentioned collecting because you have baseball practice and two or so Babe Ruth games a week. That might conflict."

"I can do it," Rain said.

"So you still want the job?"

"I want the job."

"You're sure?" Dad asked.

"I'm sure."

"Okay. You have to call that number and get an interview. My guess is that after that D.J. kid, they are going to be careful about whom they hire."

"What exactly is an interview?" Rain asked.

"The guy from the paper will ask you some questions. He wants to know if you will do a good job. So he'll ask you questions to see if you are dependable, good in school. Your job during the interview is to convince the guy that you are the best kid for the job. You will have to impress—what's the guy's name? Mr. D'Michaels. You will have to sell him on you."

"Just smile," Mom encouraged, "and you will get the job."

"Just smile?" Rain asked.

"Lots of great salespeople have great smiles has been my observation," Mom said with certainty.

"Okay, this is one ball I intend to knock out of the park," Rain declared.

And I'm going to do a lot more than smile, he thought.

CHAPTER 2

INTERVIEW
PLANNING

———

R ain wanted the paperboy job. Rain wanted to make money. Rain wanted to make money to buy things and to build up his savings. Rain intended to ace the interview and get the job. Mr. D'Michaels of *The Gazette* was coming to his house in two days to meet and interview Rain.

"Dad said I have to sell the guy," Rain remembered. "So what do I do to impress him? There are probably tons of kids applying."

Rain thought about the upcoming interview. He tried to think about how the interview might go. He figured the interview would be like a test in school. So what questions might the teacher ask, and what are the answers?

Rain made a list.

Rain's Get-the-Job Interview List

1. What questions will he ask?
2. What does he want?
3. Why should he hire me?
4. What does he need to know about me?
5. How can I be different from the other kids who apply for the job?

That night at dinner, Rain said, "Mom, Dad. I've been thinking about my interview with Mr. D'Michaels from *The Gazette*. And I'm thinking I've got to say stuff that Mr. D'Michaels wants. Any ideas?"

"If Mr. D'Michaels is on the ball, he will want from a paperboy what his customers want," Dad said. "For example, we are customers, and I want the paper delivered before I go to work, so I can read it, and leave it for Mom to read later."

"And I want the paper delivered by a handsome boy who looks just like you," Mom laughed.

Rain smiled at his mother and thought, *Handsome is not an idea. It's a fact.*

"Got it, Mom," Rain said aloud.

"I don't know about Peter and Mary Boccard on the corner. They have a business in their home. Maybe you should ask them. Can't hurt," Dad said.

"Can't hurt at all," Rain said. "Thanks!"

That's the answer, Rain thought. *That's the answer.*

CHAPTER 3

INTERVIEW

M r. D'Michaels parked his car at the curb and walked up to the front door, where Rain was already waiting.

"Hi, Rain. I'm Mr. D'Michaels."

"Nice to meet you," Rain said.

"I'm responsible for getting *The Gazette* delivered to all our customers. That means one of my jobs is to hire people to deliver the paper."

"Okay," Rain said.

"So do you have a few minutes to talk?" Mr. D'Michaels asked.

"Yes," Rain answered.

"Good. First, do you know what being a paperboy requires?"

"I think I know some stuff," Rain answered.

"Okay. Let me explain, and if it still sounds interesting to you, we can talk a bit more. All right?"

"All right," Rain said.

"Being a paperboy is not for everyone. It is physically hard work. Every day you'll be carrying a load of papers that might weigh twenty-five pounds during the week and maybe forty or more pounds on Sunday. You also have to be careful handling money. You can't misplace it. You can't get behind. Delivering papers in winter, in the cold, in the dark, causes a lot of the kids to quit. So does getting up early in the summer when there is no school. If you and your family go on vacation, it is your responsibility to have a trained kid to take your place. *The Gazette* has people who can help as problems arise, but being a paperboy is a tough job. A good job, but a tough job. What do you think?"

"I want the job." Rain said.

"Why do you want the job, Rain?"

"I want to make money."

"That's the best reason, Rain, but once again, to be sure, I have to level with you. You can make money, even a lot of money, but you will have to work for every dollar. Lot's of kids do it, so it can look easy, but it's not, especially in the beginning. Still interested?"

"Yes," Rain said.

"Okay, let's talk. How old are you?"

"Thirteen."

"What grade?"

"Seventh."

"Do you go to Towpath?"

"Yes," Rain said.

"What are your grades?" Mr. D'Michaels continued.

"Mostly A's."

"What subject is your favorite?"

"Gym."

"Besides gym," Mr. D'Michaels smiled.

"Geography. The Old West."

"How many school days a year do you think you miss for sickness or something?"

"Not many. Maybe three or four."

"Besides school classes, do you have any extra-curricular activities, like band or something?" Mr. D'Michaels asked.

"I play baseball."

"What position?"

"Third base."

"Can you think of anything, any personal stuff, anything here at your home, that might get in the way of delivering papers every day?"

"Nope."

"One last question, Rain. Do you think one of your teachers would be willing to be a reference for you?"

"What's a reference?" Rain asked.

"Someone who would vouch for you. Tell us about you in school."

"I guess so. Mrs. Kepner teaches French. Mr. Driscoll's the principal. Mr. Summers is my coach." Rain said.

"Okay, so do you have any questions for me?" Mr. D'Michaels asked.

"Do I get the job?" Rain asked.

"It looks good, Rain, but I promised I'd interview two other boys, and I would like to talk to one of those references."

"Mr. D'Michaels?" Rain asked.

"Yes?"

"I did some extra-credit work."

"You did? What did you do?" Mr. D'Michaels was curious.

"My father told me what an interview is. And I asked my dad what you might want. And my dad said that you probably want what your customers want."

"I'm with you."

"So I talked to some people around here," Rain waved, "and asked them stuff. Want to hear what they said?"

"Very interested."

"My father wants the paper delivered before he leaves for work. So does our neighbor. One lady wants the paperboy's phone number and *The Gazette's* number so she can call about wet papers, her bill—things like that. Another person asked if the paperboy could put the paper in the car when it was raining. Mr. and Mrs. Boccard want a punch card or receipt for when they paid because they forget. And Mrs. Pechter thinks the kid should carry coins and dollar bills to make change on collection day. She says she sometimes only has large bills, like tens."

Mr. D'Michaels stared in open amazement at Rain. "Rain. I am very impressed. The lady who suggested carrying money to make change: that's a new one, but obvious. That might be hard, though."

"If I can show you how to do it, will you give me the job? " Rain asked.

"Well, I do have the other interviews," Mr. D'Michaels mumbled.

Rain said nothing. He just stared at Mr. D'Michaels.

This better be good, Mr. D'Michaels thought. "Okay, Rain, what would you do?"

Rain pulled up his shirt. Attached to his belt was a silver mechanical coin changer.

"I borrowed this, but I'll get my own. It holds quarters, nickels, dimes. Just push like this, and, boom, out comes a quarter. Pretty cool, huh?"

"Pretty cool," Mr. D'Michaels agreed.

"And when you put in a coin or take out a coin it makes a little ring like a cash register," Rain explained. "A little ka-ching. So, do I get the job?"

Mr. D'Michaels thought, *I'll interview the other boys, but this is our paperboy.*

"You've got the job. Welcome to *The Gazette,*" and he extended his hand. Rain shook hands and thought to himself, *Let the ka-ching begin!*

CHAPTER 4

MONEY

———

"Congratulations, Rain. I'm happy you are on the team."

"Me too."

"Since I'm here, let's go over the money part of the job, okay? Do you know how a paperboy makes money?" asked Mr. D'Michaels.

"How?" said Rain.

"Write this down. Basically, you buy the papers from *The Gazette,* and then you sell the papers to your customers. You buy the daily papers for 15 cents apiece and sell them for 25 cents. So you make 10 cents for each paper you deliver Monday through Saturday. *The Gazette* sells you the Sunday papers for 75 cents, and you sell them for a dollar. Got it so far?"

"Perfectly," said Rain.

"The good part of this deal is that you don't have to pay *The Gazette* back until after you sell the papers. If you have forty customers and sell forty papers a day, you will owe us forty times 15 cents, or $6.00. That would be $6.00 a day. So for the Monday to Saturday papers, you would owe us $6.00 a day for six days, which is $36.00. Still with me?"

"Completely," Rain said.

"When you collect for the papers, each customer will owe you for six daily papers, which is six times 25 cents, or $1.50 for the week. When you collect from forty customers, you will collect forty times $1.50, which is $60.00. So with forty customers, you make $24 a week: the $60 you collect minus the $36 you will pay us for the papers. Do you want me to run through that again?"

"No," Rain said.

"In addition to the money you can make on the dailies you will also make 25 cents for each Sunday paper you sell. How does that sound?"

"Sounds good. Anything else?" Rain asked.

"Yes. Good paperboys often get good tips—extra money from their customers. Tips add up, especially at Christmastime, when some customers tip generously. Would you like to know what good paperboys do to earn tips?" asked Mr. D'Michaels.

"Yes," said Rain.

"Good paperboys deliver the papers on time and undamaged. Good paperboys collect weekly, keep good records, are polite and courteous. Good paperboys understand that each customer depends on *The Gazette* for news, sports, advertisements. Okay?"

"Okay," said Rain, "What else?"

"Unless the papers are delivered to you damaged, you are responsible to pay us for each paper you accept. That means if you lose some papers or deliver them to the wrong house, you still owe *The Gazette* for those papers. Our delivery driver is very good, so it is rare that you will receive bad papers. His name is Vern. Also, you have to call us if you get a new customer. And in the summertime, people go on vacation and sometimes cancel the paper for a week or two. Some people go to Florida for the whole winter. You have to let us know how many papers, including Sunday papers, you will need each week. We have a form you can use to figure out how many papers you will need. You can give the form to Vern when you pay for your papers, or you can call us. Any questions on this part?"

"Nope," Rain said.

No. Yes. Nope. This kid gets to the point, thought Mr. D'Michaels. Then he said, "Well, you should have a few. We have a very good training booklet that will show you the basics: how to fold a newspaper, keep records, fill out a customer's receipt—that kind of thing. It is very helpful. We also supply *Gazette* carry bags and receipt books.

"Okay, Rain, here is your list of customers. You will have to plan your delivery route. Vern will be here at your house at 5:30 Monday morning. He will show you how to cut the straps holding the paper bundles and how to fold and toss a paper. Listen to Vern. He's a good guy and was a great paperboy," Mr. D'Michaels said.

"So I'm a paperboy?" Rain asked.

"To me," said Mr. D'Michaels, "you will not be a true paperboy until you have done the job for one year. When will you be fourteen?"

"Next June," Rain answered.

"If you are still working for *The Gazette* next June, then you will be a paperboy. Do you think you can make it? Lots of kids bigger than you have quit."

"Yes, I can make it. And Mr. D'Michaels, as you explained it, I buy the papers from *The Gazette* and the customers pay me. Correct?"

"Correct."

"So if I buy from *The Gazette*, and I sell and deliver the papers, and the customers pay me, and then I pay you, why do you say I'm working for *The Gazette?*

As I see it, I'm working for the people who pay me," Rain said.

Mr. D'Michaels smiled. "You make a good point."

"Thank you for the job. Now, don't go out of business on me. Lots of newspapers bigger than you have quit," Rain joked.

"We won't quit," Mr. D'Michaels replied.

"Good," Rain said. "See you next June."

CHAPTER 5

THE DINNER TABLE

"How did your interview with the man from *The Gazette* go?" Rain's dad asked.

"It went great. His name is Mr. D'Michaels. I got the job. I start next Monday."

"That's wonderful, Rain," Rain's mom said. "You will be a great paperboy."

"Would you like me to drive you on your route the first day?" Dad asked.

"I don't think so. I'm going to do a practice run tomorrow," Rain said.

"Great idea," Mom said. "Rain, take some more carrots and broccoli. They'll help you pedal."

Pedal? C'mon, Mom! Rain thought. "Okay, Mom," he said aloud.

"Rain," Dad said, "a paperboy is not just any job. You are your own boss. You work for yourself. Your route is exactly like having your own business. And it's one of the few jobs that the politicians haven't yet figured out a way to tax you, to make you pay some of your money to the government."

"What do you mean, 'own business'?" Rain asked.

"It means that a paperboy is a business owner, a businessman."

"Dad, do you mean I'm not just a paperboy, I'm a businessman?" Rain asked.

"One thing's for sure: if you succeed as a morning paperboy, you will indeed be a businessman even if you are only thirteen," Dad said.

"Maybe you are a businessboy," Mom said.

Geez, Mom, Rain thought.

"Do you know how you are going to make money?" Dad asked.

"Yes. Mr. D'Michaels explained how I buy papers for fifteen cents and sell them for twenty-five cents. It's pretty easy," Rain said.

"Rain, please pass Dad some more meatloaf," Mom said. "I think all the people on your route will like you and will give you tips. And you know where some of your best tips will come?"

"From who?" Rain asked.

"From whom," Mom corrected. "Your best tips will come from your favorite customers: Dad and me."

"I'll hold you to that!" Rain said.

"What did the man tell you about forecasting?" Dad asked.

"Forecasting? Like checking the weather?" Rain answered.

"In business, forecasting is predicting future sales so the business will have enough time to be able to supply whatever it sells. For you, it means having the correct number of papers so that no customer goes without. It also means not having extra papers, which you can't sell but have to pay for," Dad explained.

"Yes, he did explain that, but he didn't call it forecasting," Rain said.

"Well, if you're going to be a businessman, or as Mom says, a businessboy, we should talk about business subjects, don't you think?" Dad suggested.

"I'm game," Raid said.

"Well, I'm not so game. That's enough business talk for tonight," Mom said. "Who wants lemon meringue pie for dessert?"

"I'm game," Dad said.

"I'm game," Rain said.

CHAPTER 6

DAY ONE

I t was 5:15 A.M., and Rain was waiting at the foot of his driveway. He was meeting *The Gazette* delivery man at 5:30. He bounced back and forth in his black low-cut sneakers.

I hope I can do this, he thought.

Even though he had ridden his route a couple of times, Rain kept looking at the map he had drawn.

I can definitely do this, he said to himself. *Definitely.*

He heard the truck before he saw it.

In seconds, two headlights crawled down his street.

"This is it," Rain said aloud to himself.

The truck came to a stop. The driver's door opened, and a big guy glided onto the street. The big guy held out his hand. "You must be Rain. My name is Vern. Nice to meet ya."

Rain shook Vern's hand. "Nice to meet you too."

"Okay," Vern said. "Let's get at it."

And Rain's training began.

Vern explained that it was easier to cut the big bands that held the paper stacks together with scissors than with a knife. "Knives slip and cut the front page. Scissors don't, plus they cut better."

"These are your *Gazette* carry bags." Vern said. "They have straps so you can carry them on your shoulder. You've got a bike. That's good. We can fit the bags to your bike. If you get stuck, you can pull a wagon loaded with papers."

Pull a wagon, Rain thought. *What? Like a little red wagon with "Kindergarten" painted on the side?*

"Okay," he said aloud.

Vern showed Rain how to fold the papers. "If you get them tight like this, they are easier to toss. Easier to put in *The Gazette* tubes. And you put them in the bags like this. Straight up and down. You get more in, and they're easier to grab."

"Got it," Rain said.

"Good," Vern said. "Okay fold this one. Then toss it toward the truck. See if you can land it on the hood."

Rain folded the paper, not as tightly as did Vern, but exactly as did Vern. He threw the paper at the truck. It landed on the middle of the hood, next to the windshield.

"Nice throw," Vern said.

"I play baseball," Rain said.

Yes, I know, Vern thought to himself.

"Okay, Rain, I think you are ready. Do you want me to follow you for a few houses?" Vern asked.

"No, thank you, Vern. I can do it."

"Okay, kid. Oh, one more thing. You might get tired the first few days. That's common. Guys aren't used to pedaling a heavy bike, and this bike is loaded. If you get tired, take a break. Your customers won't mind if they get their paper a little late. For the last couple of months, they were lucky to even get the paper."

"Okay," Rain said.

"Good luck, kid."

Rain watched until the truck's rear lights disappeared.

From the first second, just getting his bike started, the route was torture. The slightest hill required all of Rain's strength. He left his bike at the bottom of Wellington Heights and delivered those papers on foot.

It took Rain over three hours to deliver the papers. He missed some houses and had to go back. He made bad throws and had to get off his bike and find the paper and get it close to the customer's porch. Mangy mutts chased him, trying to nip at his legs. He legs burned from pedaling.

When he finally got back to his house, his butt hurt, his legs hurt, his throwing arm hurt, and his shirt was soaked with sweat. He flopped on his bed and allowed himself an almost silent groan. *I'm dead*, he thought, before he fell asleep.

That night at the dinner table, Dad asked Rain, "So how did your first day go?"

"It was brutal. It took forever. I don't know, Dad."

"It's hard pedaling all that weight, isn't it?" Dad asked.

"Horrible," Rain said, shaking his head.

"It gets easier," Dad said.

"I don't know," Rain muttered.

"Would you like me to drive you tomorrow?" Mom asked.

"I don't know," Rain answered, head down.

Dad glanced at Mom. "Rain. Look at me," Dad said.

Rain looked up. "There are two things you do know. You know being a paperboy is a tough job. And you know you can't quit. Not after one day."

Rain kept silent.

"Your mother offered to drive you. Or you can use your bike. Okay?" Dad said.

"Okay."

"Okay, what?" Dad asked.

"I'll use my bike."

"Rain. All that pedaling and pulling will make you stronger for baseball," Mom said.

Rain looked at his smiling mother and thought to himself, *If I live long enough.*

"And Rain, I have a delivery idea for you," Mom said. "Do the houses on Wellington Heights last, when your bag is almost empty. That is a fairly big hill."

Try Mount Everest, Rain thought.

"I am definitely doing Wellington Heights last," Raid said aloud.

"And going downhill is easier," Mom said.

"Yup," Rain agreed.

"This is your favorite," Mom said as she passed a plate of chicken.

An hour after dinner, Rain said he was going to bed.

"Oh, Rain. I almost forgot," Mom said. "Mrs. Christopher called. She wanted me to thank you for putting the note on her paper introducing yourself and giving your telephone number. She said she is looking forward to thanking you in person."

"Thanks, Mom."

"Maybe you'll earn a lot of tips," Mom suggested.

"Okay, Mom," Rain said.

As Rain trudged up the stairs, he thought, *Yeah, a lot of tips. Maybe I can buy myself a tombstone.*

CHAPTER 7

MEAN DOGS

Everybody who makes their living delivering things to people's homes knows about dogs. Dogs bite mail carriers. Dogs bite delivery people. Dogs in the house are okay. Dogs outside the house are not. Unleashed dogs outside the house in the early morning darkness are super not okay. Some dogs chase cars. Some dogs chase kids on bikes. Some dogs come flying out of the dark without warning to attack the rider.

Rain's route consisted of fifty-six homes located on six neighborhood streets. The route was about five miles of flat streets with one fairly big hill. The houses were generally near the street, although it was not uncommon for Rain to pedal up and down driveways to deliver the papers. Scattered along the route there were many dogs. Most were nice, but the mean dogs, especially those that roamed outside, were a big problem.

Rain didn't know who owned the dogs, so he couldn't notify the owners. The dogs would race alongside his bike, ferociously barking and growling and trying to bite Rain's legs. Rain yelled at the dogs and waved a newspaper at them, but mostly he would try to outrace them. Rain didn't know what to do, so he visited the Bike Rack, a local store that sold everything cyclists needed. Rain told the fellow in the store his problem. The fellow told Rain that most dogs attack because they think the biker is invading their territory. The bike expert gave Rain some advice and a number of suggestions.

Over the next few days when a dog came running out, Rain got off his bike, keeping the bike between him and the dog. He then said, "My name is Rain," and calmly squirted the dog with cold water from a water gun. Just as the bike expert predicted, dogs don't like to get water on their faces, and after two or three soakings, even the dimmest of dogs stopped chasing.

Unleashed mean dogs caged behind customer fences were a different problem. Rain's strategy was to make friends with those dogs. He reasoned that the dogs loved their owners, so he could make them love him. He gave the dogs treats, and soon the dogs looked forward to Rain's daily visit. The mean dogs quickly became nice dogs.

Except one.

One dog was crazy mean. The dog was a big, vicious beast, and larger than Rain. The first day Rain delivered to the beast's house, the dog launched himself against the fence, growling fiercely and snapping his jaws. The dog kept leaping at the fence, terrifying Rain. Afraid to get too close, Rain left the newspaper outside the fence. Some nights later the beast's owner called Rain to complain that the newspaper should be left inside the fence. Rain said the dog tried to kill him. Rain told the owner he would put the newspaper anywhere the customer wanted if the dog were on a chain leash or inside the house. The owner told Rain the dog was all bark and no bite and to leave the paper inside the fence.

The next morning, Rain folded the newspaper, tied it with a string, and threw it over the fence. The beast immediately raced to the paper, sniffed it, and then ripped it to shreds. That night the dog's owner again called to complain. "The paper was destroyed," said the dog's owner. Rain told the owner that the dog wanted to kill him, and the dog's attack on the paper was proof. The owner told Rain that he must have done something to antagonize the dog. Rain asked the owner to watch tomorrow morning and see for himself. The next morning, Rain tied the paper and threw it over the fence. Rain watched as once again, the dog pounced on the paper, ripping it to pieces. The owner burst from the house yelling at the dog, but it was too late. By the time the owner got to the fence, his daily newspaper was confetti.

"Okay, Rain, tomorrow the dog will be in the house," the owner said.

At dinner, Rain's mom asked if he needed any more raw hamburger to make friends with the mean dog. "I don't need any more, Mom. That dog must be starving. That dog will go through anything to get food. I can deliver the guy's paper tomorrow with no problem."

CHAPTER 8

THE TEN CUSTOMER COMMANDMENTS

———

R ain learned that his customers liked him, but that they liked getting their papers more. Rain learned that his customers weren't interested in why their paper didn't show up, or didn't show up on time. Moses had his Ten Commandments. They were God's commandments on how people should treat each other. Rain had ten other commandments: his customers' commandments as to how Rain should treat them.

> *Thou shalt not fail to deliver.*
> *Thou shalt not be late.*
> *Thou shalt not be sick.*
> *Thou shalt not be on vacation.*

Thou shalt not be in camp.

Thou shalt not deliver wet, damaged,
*   or incomplete papers.*

Thou shalt not have bike trouble.

Thou shalt not get lost.

Thou shalt not be tired.

Thou shalt not make excuses.

CHAPTER 9

THE SUNDAYS

——

S undays were killer paperboy days. The Sunday
newspaper was five times as big as the daily.
"The Sundays," as Rain called them, were big and
bad. The Sundays could weigh 40 to 50 pounds. Rain
weighed 115 pounds. Rain had rigged his bike with two
bags, each able to hold about thirty dailies, enough to
do his weekday route on one trip. On Sundays Rain had
to load papers, deliver, bike home, reload, deliver, bike
home . . . two or three times.

When delivering the Monday through Saturday
papers, Rain could prefold, tie, and toss many of them
while moving on his bike. For the rest of the papers, he
could skid to a one-foot stop, put the paper in the *Gazette*
cylinder, and move on. Folding and throwing the Sunday papers was impossible. The papers were too big, too
unwieldy, too heavy. So for every Sunday customer, Rain

had to get off his bike and carry the Sunday monster up to the house.

One Sunday there was a blustering rain and wind storm. It was hard enough for Rain to pedal the Sunday papers with no wind. It was murder when there was a gale.

Rain had fifteen papers left to deliver. He put his bike on the kickstand, grabbed a monster, and jogged up the customer's driveway. As Rain dropped the paper on the customer's porch, he heard a strong wind blow over his precariously balanced bike. The wind immediately started blowing the papers apart, scattering them over the road. Rain raced to his bike to save his papers, but the wind was wicked. He'd grab a clump of papers, put them under his bike, turn to get other loose papers, only to have the wind whip the captured papers apart.

Rain was frantic. He owed *The Gazette* for the papers no matter what. His money was literally blowing away. His customers would be angry. Rain scraped his knuckles and broke some nails scraping out rocks and fallen branches from the side of the road. He put the rocks and sticks on each pile of random sections of papers. Fighting to catch his breath, Rain outran the flailing wind. He went after the important parts of the paper first, especially the front pages and the sports section. He read the sports pages and the comics, so he figured his customers did as well. The devil wind offered bad options: Get the reading sections or get the advertising inserts? He chose the reading sections, and the wind blew coupons and "Going Out of Business Sale" notices into the woods, culverts, and nearby lawns.

Using rocks and fallen tree branches, Rain eventually rescued most of the Sundays. Slowly, painfully, he reassembled the Sunday monsters as best as possible. Many were smudged, had ripped and wrinkled pages, and were missing sections.

Rain was upset. He wanted to quit and go home. But his paper route was his business, and these papers belonged to his customers. Rain wondered what his favorite customers such as his mother and father and Mr. and Mrs. Burrows down the street would think about this week's Sunday paper. He took his pen from his customer record and receipt notebook, and on the top of the front page of every remaining paper wrote:

Damaged Newspaper. Discount available. Rain, Your Paperboy.

Rain didn't blame the wind. He didn't make excuses. The paper is delivered on time, or it's not. Period.

That night Rain sat down to think hard about his Sunday monster problem. The Sundays were too big to fold, but something clearly had to be done. He vowed never to have another Black Sunday. He decided to buy strong string or huge rubber bands to hold the papers together.

The next morning, Monday, he was up even earlier than the hated 5:30 A.M. to meet Vern. He gave Vern two other addresses and asked him if he would please divide up his fifty-six Sunday papers and make two additional drops—three altogether. One stop was on the top of Wellington Heights. The extra stops were extra work for Vern, but Rain was a good little kid and Vern liked him. And the idea made sense, Vern agreed. Rain thanked Vern and told him, "If you do the same thing for some of the other kids, lots more Sundays will be delivered earlier, making lots of customers happier. That will be good for *The Gazette*." Vern wrote up Rain's idea and dropped it into *The Gazette's* suggestion box. Rain and Vern each received a nice thank-you letter from *The Gazette's* publisher.

Rain didn't learn until twelve years later, when he was in graduate business school, that his three-drop concept was called *supply chain management*.

Not one customer asked Rain for a discount. The next week, in the afternoon before baseball practice, when Rain was going to the homes collecting the week's money, several customers commended him on his "damage and discount" note. Mrs. Burrows said, "Rain, your note brought sunshine into this house." She gave him a dollar tip.

CHAPTER 10

REFERRALS

———

Once Rain started making and saving money, he wanted to make more. And to do that, he needed to sell more papers. To sell more papers, Rain needed more customers. Rain focused on ways to get more customers.

He put flyers in the mailboxes and on the porches of potential customers, but he was disappointed with the results of his flyer campaign. For every fifty flyers, he might get one new customer. He didn't have the money to advertise. With school and sports and homework, he didn't have the time to go door to door and sell. What to do?

Rain studied his customer list. He studied and studied. Then, eureka! He found the clue: almost all of his newest customers had called Rain at the suggestion of another customer. Rain later learned in a business class in college that one customer talking to another customer is called *word-of-mouth advertising*.

Rain wondered if he could get more customers to talk to their neighbors about their great paperboy. He couldn't come up with a good idea to make that happen. Then he wondered, What if he were to act as a go-between—the person between a current customer and a possible new one? He worked on this idea. Rain was going to ask his nice customers for the name of a neighbor who wasn't getting *The Gazette*. Then Rain would introduce himself to the potential new customer, mention the neighbor's name, and ask if this potential customer wanted daily delivery. Rain then talked to Vern, because he would need *The Gazette*'s help.

Rain usually visited his customers to collect the weekly bill on afternoons. From experience, he knew that more of his customers were home on Sunday afternoons than other days. He usually did not have a baseball game on Sundays. He liked collecting the money because that's when he got paid for his papers and received tips from many of his customers. Collecting money on Sundays also took the sting out of delivering the monster Sundays.

On this Sunday, Rain planned to ask five customers to give him the names of possible new customers. His first customer was Mrs. Speath.

"Hello, Mrs. Speath," said Rain, "Your bill for the week is $2.50: $1.50 for the daily papers and $1.00 for Sunday."

"Thank you, Rain. Here is $3.00. Please keep the change," Mrs. Speath said.

"Thank you very much. Oh, and Mrs. Speath," Rain asked, "do you know anyone in the neighborhood who might like to get *The Gazette?*"

"Gee, Rain, I don't really know who gets or doesn't get the paper," Mrs. Speath said.

"How about Mr. and Mrs. Doyle? They don't get the paper," Rain suggested.

"Really? Well they are very nice people, and I'm sure they would be interested," Mrs. Speath said.

"Thanks a lot, Mrs. Speath," Rain said, and off he went.

A few minutes later, Rain rang the doorbell at the Doyle house.

A women answered the door. "Hello," she said.

"Are you Mrs. Doyle?" Rain asked.

"Yes, I am. And who are you?" Mrs. Doyle asked.

Rain answered, "I'm Rain. I go to Towpath Middle School. My parents live on Bruce Lane, two streets over. I deliver *The Gazette* to people on this street. I talked to Mrs. Speath. She said you might be interested in getting *The Gazette*. If you are, you can get one week of papers free. To see if you like it. You will get the paper every day before 7:00 A.M. and before 8:00 A.M. on Sundays. Would you like to give it a try?" Rain asked.

"Well, how do you do. Rain? Nice to meet you," Mrs. Doyle said. "My children went to Towpath years ago. We used to get *The Gazette*. I forgot why we don't anymore. Maybe we cancelled when we went on vacation. I don't know. How much is the paper?"

"Your first week is free. The paper is twenty-five cents a day Monday though Saturday. The Sunday paper is a dollar. The delivery is also free. Is that okay?" Rain asked.

"That is more than okay, Rain. When could you deliver the first paper?" Mrs. Doyle asked.

"Probably Tuesday," Rain answered.

"Okay, Rain. That is fine. You have a new customer," Mrs. Doyle said.

"Thanks a lot. See you soon," Rain said.

Yes! thought the fist-pumping Rain. *A new customer! My idea works!*

Rain called on five other prospects. The first two said, "No, thanks." The third wasn't home. The last two said yes. Rain was good in math. He calculated that fifty flyers might generate one customer. He compared handing out flyers to this new idea of getting six names, which resulted in three new customers. Getting names was a way better selling strategy than sticking flyers in mail boxes.

That Sunday night, he called *The Gazette* delivery driver. Rain told Vern, "I'll need three extra papers tomorrow. We have three new customers! I told them they would probably get their papers on Tuesday, but I want to surprise them tomorrow. And, Vern, thanks for getting *The Gazette* to spring for the one week of free papers."

Vern said, "That's good news. Congratulations Rain. You might be a rainmaker."

"What is a rainmaker?" Rain asked.

"A rainmaker is someone who brings in new business, brings in new customers. A rainmaker is someone who helps the customer and thereby makes money for *The Gazette* and for himself," Vern explained.

Sitting at his little desk in his little bedroom, writing in his record and planning notebook, Rain scheduled the three new customers into his route. He now had fifty-nine customers. Rain liked making money. If rainmakers made money, then that's what he would be. He would make it rain.

Rain's radio was on. The weather forecast for tomorrow predicted heavy rain. "I hate it when it rains," Rain groused.

But he set his alarm and climbed into bed.

CHAPTER 11

THE CONTEST

S lipped under the strap that held together his bun-
dle of papers was a large envelope addressed to
Rain. Inside was a large, colorful flyer announcing and
describing the "Summer Time. Selling Time" paperboy
sales contest. There were pictures of various prizes
including the first prize, a hundred dollar U.S. Savings
Bond. The rules were simple: the five paperboys or
papergirls who sold the most new, additional papers, over
and above their route's current number of customers,
would win. The contest would be held the second and
third weeks of July. Most of the routes had about the
same number of customers, forty to sixty. If the kid
selling fifty papers a day sold an additional twelve, and
everyone else sold fewer than twelve, that first kid won.

Rain wanted that savings bond, and he knew he
had to come up with a good selling idea. Distributing

flyers produced only one or two new customers, and he had to first write, print, and deliver at least a hundred flyers. His idea to get one customer to suggest another was good, but it took forever to get the names, meet the people, and get the sale. The contest started in two weeks, and then he had only two weeks to increase his sales.

How do I sell more papers? Where can I sell more papers? thought Rain. *Let's start,* he thought, *with where I* can't *sell papers. I can't sell papers to people who already get the paper at home. I can't sell papers to people who buy them at a local store. I can't stand on a street corner like the kids in the old movies shouting, "Read all about it" because I don't live in a city. I can't walk down the middle of a street full of traffic selling papers, like the guys do in front of Yankee Stadium, because my parents would go berserk. How do I sell? Where do I sell?*

The contest started in a few days. On some mornings during the summer, Rain did not ride his bike directly home. If he didn't have to go to school, there was no rush to get home. Instead, he would ride his bike to the diner in the center of his small town to get a Coke. The diner was owned by a Greek family with a last name that was fun to pronounce but impossible to spell. The name was "Papadopolous." Everyone called the owner "Pops" and called his wife "Mrs. Pops." At 7:00 in the morning, the diner was always busy. All kinds of people were having breakfast or getting coffee and food to eat in their cars on their way to work.

Rain parked his bike in a safe spot near the diner and walked to the entrance. Lined up in front of the diner were four self-serve newspaper boxes. The customer put in the money and took out a paper. As Rain neared the diner, he watched a guy put in some money and instead of reaching into the box for his paper, the man took the last paper displayed on the box door. The guy then walked into the diner. Rain looked at the four boxes. The boxes holding the *Times* and the *Journal* had papers in the window on the front of the box door. The boxes holding *the Post* and Rain's *Gazette* were empty. Sold out!

A woman appeared next to Rain, looked at the empty *Gazette* box, and said, "Darn! I'm too late again. Why doesn't that stupid *Gazette* fill the box with more papers or put up another box? This is ridiculous." She got into a waiting van and exclaimed to the other passengers, "No paper today!"

Rain watched the car pool leave. It looked as if there were five or six people in the van. Five or six people who might have bought *The Gazette*! In the next fifteen minutes, Rain counted eleven people who first looked at the empty *Gazette* box and then bought the *New York Times*, or no paper at all. Rain was excited as he went into Pops's diner.

"Good morning, Rain," Mrs. Pops said.

"Hi," Rain said.

"What would you like today?" Mrs. Pops asked.

"A Coke, please," Rain answered.

Putting the Coke on the counter, Mrs. Pops said, "You should be drinking milk, Rain."

Rain looked at her. "Mrs. Pops," he began, "I have a business idea for you."

"You do, do you? What is it?" she asked.

"I've noticed that lots of people buy a newspaper in the outside boxes and then come into your diner to read the paper and get stuff to eat. I've also noticed that when the boxes have no papers, people look at the empty box and drive away. I'll bet that if *The Gazette* box had more papers, more people would buy a paper and then come inside," Rain said.

"I never thought of that before, but you are probably right," Mrs. Pops said. "But what about this business proposal?"

"I'm a paperboy," Rain stated.

"I know," Mrs. Pops said.

"I was thinking that if I sold *The Gazette* to your customers after *The Gazette* box was empty, you would get more customers," said Rain.

Mrs. Pops smiled at Rain. "Rain, do you know that *The Gazette* pays us to let them put their paper box out in front?"

"Do they pay you for the papers sold or just for the box?" Rain asked.

"Just for the box, I guess," she said.

"How about this?" Rain asked, "I'll sell papers in your parking lot for two weeks. At the end of the two weeks, I'll tell you and Pops how many I sold. Then you can call *The Gazette* and tell them if they should put another box here. *The Gazette* will sell that number of extra papers. Then you can get more money for the new box and get more people coming in to buy breakfast."

"Hey, Pops! Got a sec?" Mrs. Pops shouted. "Rain here has a business proposal, and I think we should do it."

She explained Rain's idea to Pops. Pops looked at Rain and said, "When you turn sixteen, if you want a job here in the diner, you've got one. When can you start selling papers and getting more people into our diner?"

"Monday morning."

"Okay, Rain," Pops said as he stuck out his hand, "we have a deal." Rain shook hands with Pops and Mrs. Pops.

"May I please have another Coke?" Rain asked.

"Yes, you may, and it's on the house," Mrs. Pops said.

CHAPTER 12

LUCK

"Rain, congratulations on winning the savings bond!" Dad said. "Selling at Pops's diner was a creative idea."

"I am so glad I went to Pops that day," Rain said. "What luck! I was running out of time before the contest started. When I was over at Ellis's house playing catch, he said I was born under a lucky star."

"Why do you say it was luck? Paper boxes are empty everywhere. Every other kid could have seen that. But only you saw the opportunity, and you made the deal with Pops. That is not luck, Rain, that is entrepreneurship," Dad said.

"It's what?" Rain asked.

"Entrepreneurship. Being an entrepreneur. Entrepreneurs start new companies. They see opportunities where others see problems. Most small business owners like Pops are entrepreneurs," Dad said.

"Not just luck?" Rain asked.

"There are all kinds of luck. The worst luck is what attracts people to bet money in a gambling casino. If you put money in a slot machine and you win, that is pure luck—something you can't control," Dad said.

"Speaking of luck," Mom said, "I was lucky to find this sweet corn at that the farm stand today. Isn't it delicious?"

"It's great, Mom."

"See, I don't think Mom was lucky to find this corn on the cob," said Dad. "If Mom didn't get in her car and purposefully drive to the farm, she wouldn't have been so lucky. Mom made her own luck, and now we are the lucky ones.

"Rain, all your life, you are going to meet people who will complain about having bad luck and who say that other people 'get all the luck.' You will meet other people who are successful, who are winners. And because they are modest and know accomplishing big things is rarely easy, they will say they are lucky," Dad said.

"What about the lottery, Dad? The ads say you can't win if you don't play."

"Right, but there are no ads saying you will most likely lose every single time you play." Rain's father knew Rain hated to lose. "Only bet on yourself. Only bet on people you trust. Only bet on your ideas. Then you will be lucky," Dad said.

"Your father and I see how hard you are working, even though I practically had to drag you out of bed this morning. So here is a bonus, a surprise," Mom said, as she handed him an envelope.

Inside the envelope was another hundred-dollar savings bond. "Wow! Thanks, Mom. Thanks, Dad."

"Study hard and save some money, and you will be very lucky," Dad said.

"Rain, please do the dishes, and take the garbage out," Mom said.

"Mom, the baseball game is starting on channel 8," Rain pleaded.

"Then get going, and you won't miss much," Mom said.

It was just getting dark as Rain hustled the trash barrel to the street. In the sky, Rain saw a bright star. (It was actually the planet Venus, but Rain wouldn't take astronomy until ninth grade.)

Hey, Rain thought. *Maybe Ellis is right.*

"Move it, Rain," he urged himself. "Move it. The baseball game is on." And Rain raced up the driveway, tapping his back pocket once to be sure the savings bond was still there.

CHAPTER 13

BONUS

———

M r. D'Michaels, who ran the circulation department at *The Gazette*, called Rain. "Rain, I've got some good news. Vern turned in your idea, and you are getting a twenty-five-dollar bonus."

"Wow! Thanks," Rain said. "But I didn't turn in any ideas."

"After winning the "Summer Time. Selling Time" contest, you told Vern that maybe we should have someone watch all *The Gazette*'s newspaper boxes to see if they were filled with enough papers, to see if we were running out and losing sales. And thanks to your idea, we are now selling over two hundred additional papers every day. Congratulations again," Mr. D'Michaels said.

"Thanks," Rain said. "But Vern turned in the idea. Shouldn't he get the bonus?"

"Don't worry about Vern. He's always winning something. I told you before that Vern is a good guy. In my opinion, he knows everything about selling papers, but he says he learns new things all the time. Vern has been with *The Gazette* for a long time, so when he recommends someone for a bonus, we take it seriously."

"How long has Vern worked for *The Gazette?*" Rain asked.

"We counted his years as a paperboy, when he was like you. And last year there was a nice celebration and a plaque and a gold Rolex—the whole bit—to thank Vern for sixty years of service."

"Sixty years! That's older than my father," Rain exclaimed.

"Yup. Vern has delivered more papers than there are stars in the skies," said Mr. D'Michaels. "Oh, and Rain, Vern has a nickname for you. He calls you his 'Little Rainmaker.'"

"At *The Gazette?*"

"Yes, he does. You should get your twenty-five dollars in a day or so. Keep up the good work!"

The next morning, tacked to a tomato stake, was an envelope addressed to Vern that he could not miss. Inside was a note that read:

Dear Vern:

Thank you for getting me the $25 bonus.
I can use the money.

Deliveringly yours,
Rain, your paperboy

Vern read the note and thought, *I've been delivering papers all my life, and I can count the paperboy thank-you notes on one hand. This kid is definitely a rainmaker.*

CHAPTER 14

THE BULLY
(PART I)

———

For two weeks every August, Rain's parents rented a cottage at the beach. Because it was his father's annual vacation, Rain knew not to complain that he would miss a few baseball games. Besides, Rain loved the beach. He always met other kids, and they would play baseball in the sand, go crabbing, have mud fights on the sandbars. The big problem was to find a kid who was willing to take over his paper route for two weeks. The year before, Rain's first August, Vern had delivered the papers for the two weeks. This was Rain's first time hiring a substitute.

Finding a kid was hard. Most kids didn't want to get up at 5:30 A.M., or were also on vacation, or physically couldn't do the job. At first Rain thought he would split the profit fifty-fifty with his sub, but decided that the more money someone could make, the easier it would be to find someone who would cover his route. Rain figured that giving another kid two weeks' profit to get his papers delivered was worth it.

Chuckie Moriarty agreed to deliver Rain's papers. Chuckie was fifteen, two years older than Rain, and lived a few streets over. Rain didn't know him well, but both boys were in the same school district. Rain knew Chuck was big and good at sports. He figured he would have no problem with the Sunday papers.

Rain spent a morning showing Chuckie how to do everything. They rode their bikes along Rain's route. Rain made a map with his customers' names printed inside little drawings of houses. Rain explained to Chuckie how the money worked.

"When you collect, the people will give you money for the papers and maybe a tip. Put any tip money you get in this envelope. That's 100 percent your money. You keep all the tip money. Put all the other collection money in this *Gazette* envelope. When I get home, I will subtract the money I owe *The Gazette* for the papers and give you the rest. So you will get all the tips and all the profits. Okay?"

"Okay," Chuckie agreed.

Because Rain's bike was outfitted with *The Gazette* delivery bags, the deal included letting Chuckie use

57

Rain's bike for the two weeks. Rain told Chuckie about Vern and the 5:30 A.M. paper drops.

Rain told Vern about Chuckie and left for vacation.

Two weeks later, Rain returned and walked over to Chuckie's house. Rain's bike was lying near Chuckie's garage. It was covered in mud, with one flat tire, some broken wheel spokes, and a missing seat.

"What happened to my bike?" Rain exclaimed.

"Some kid stole it. I just found it by the street yesterday," Chuckie answered.

Rain was quiet for a moment. "Why," he asked, "would someone steal a bike with big canvas bags?"

"Who knows? Who cares?" Chuckie said.

"All right. Let's count the money," Rain said.

"Here's the money," Chuckie said.

Rain counted the money. He looked up at Chuckie.

"Chuckie, this is not enough money. This isn't even half of what you should have collected. I don't think there is enough here to pay *The Gazette*."

"That's not my problem, pal. Lots of people weren't home and didn't pay. And I already took my share of the money."

Chuckie was at least three inches taller and thirty pounds heavier than Rain. Looking down at Rain,

Chuckie jammed his fist into Rain's chest, saying, "Now get lost."

Rain stumbled. Then Chuckie shoved Rain, knocking him down.

"Hope you had a nice vacation, dork," Chuckie said. Rain heard Chuckie laughing as he ambled to his house and slammed the door.

Rain pushed his broken bike home. His chest was killing him. Tears smeared his face. He felt humiliated and helpless. He was afraid. And he smoldered.

Later that day and over the next day, Rain learned that the bully Chuckie was a big-time thief and liar. There were messages from customers who didn't receive all their papers, including the Sundays. Vern said some people called *The Gazette* saying they got their papers the first week but always late—sometimes in the afternoon. Many people did not get all the dailies or the Sundays in the second week.

Vern said that *The Gazette* was very upset with Rain, especially because Rain was one of *The Gazette*'s outstanding paperboys.

Rain called all his customers and learned that almost all his customers paid Chuckie for the first week. A few customers did not pay Chuckie the second week: they wanted to speak to Rain first. Rain wrote a note to every customer apologizing for what happened while he was gone. He promised each customer a free makeup paper for each undelivered paper, including any missed Sundays. Although *The Gazette* charged Rain only half-price for the makeup papers, Chuckie cost him a lot of money. Rain added up the money to fix his bike, plus the cost of the makeup papers, plus the money he had to pay *The Gazette*, plus what Chuckie stole, and it came out to $142.40.

Rain's mom and dad were furious, but Rain insisted they not call Chuckie's parents. "Unfortunately, Rain," Dad said, "this is a bitter lesson. But you are not alone. Even good experienced companies hire the wrong people, and the wrong people cost companies lots of money."

"I didn't realize," Mom said, "that Chuckie was such a loser. But just think Rain: there are fifty-nine families that now know what kind of person you are and what a loser Chuckie is. Believe me, it will catch up to him."

Vern knew what happened. He told Rain, "You are not the only person to go through this. The same thing happened to me."

"What did you do?" Rain asked.

"I didn't make the same hiring mistake twice. And sometimes things even out. Bullies don't pick on just one kid. Who knows, someday he might pick on the wrong kid. Karma will get him in the end. Don't worry."

Rain nodded.

CHAPTER 15

GREEN
LIGHTNING

——

During daylight savings time, it was light at 5:30 A.M. when Rain started his paper route. As summer moved to fall, the mornings got darker earlier and earlier. Fog or rain or snow could make any morning pitch black. Rain needed a spotlight on his bike to see where he was going, and he needed lights or reflectors so that drivers could see him. Rain's father said he would pay for the lights, but Rain had to install them.

Rain didn't know the difference between a screwdriver and a pile driver. But his good friend Ellis was a mechanical wizard and knew the difference. Rain told Ellis what he wanted and offered to pay. Ellis said no to the money: he was in it for the challenge. And a challenge it was. Two weeks later, Rain's bike glowed like a carnival ride. It had dual spotlights, bright green flashing lights that spun with the wheels, smaller lights that went around with the pedals, and special lights that illuminated the canvas carrier bags. It had three-toned horns and sirens. A big American flag was attached to the back fender.

"This is awesome, outstanding, perfect!" Rain exclaimed. "It is *exactly* what I was looking for."

"You said you wanted them to see you coming and going a mile away. You said you wanted as many lights as Idi Amin's Jeep had flags. This baby is cooler than the light show at Teen Club," beamed the proud inventor. "This little number is festooned!"

"Festooned, my man, festooned!" Rain chorused. "And I love those green lights on the wheels."

"Yeah, green and fast," Ellis said. "Green lightning!"

"Ellis. This bike is now named Green Lightning!"

Rain's light-show bicycle was all about visibility: visibility for safety and visibility for business. Green Lightning was an out-there, unforgettable neon sign advertising Rain and *The Gazette*.

It was also good business for Ellis.

Every kid in town wanted a bike like Rain's. Rain told each kid who asked where he got his lights to call Ellis. Kids flocked to Ellis, who charged each kid to hot-light his or her bike. Soon there were lots of bikes with lights and sound in town. Ellis asked Rain if he cared if there were copycats running around.

"Nope," said Rain. "Between 5:30 and 7:00 A.M., there is only one light show on the road, and that's me and Green Lightning. Maybe the other guys will remind people to remember their paperboy . . . especially on collection day."

"Yeah. Good thinking. And by the way," Ellis asked, "who is Idi Amin?"

CHAPTER 16

INNOVATION

———

R ain raced down the street on his cool new bike. With his right hand, he reached behind his seat and pulled out a prefolded newspaper. As he did every morning, Rain flipped the paper toward the customer's front door. But unlike other mornings, the paper didn't land kerplunk on the porch. A tall man casually caught the missile in mid flight. "Hey, Rain," he called, "gotta sec?"

"Hi," Rain said.

"Good morning, Rain," the customer said. "I need a favor. My wife and I both travel a lot in our work. It's hard to predict our schedule, so there's no sense in canceling the paper, then restarting. What I'm hoping you might do is wrap our papers in a bag or plastic or something so they don't get ruined when we are away. And also, would you mind delivering the paper to our back door? We'd be happy to pay you extra. We just don't want newspapers all over the front yard. That would signal to people that no one is home. Can you do it?"

"Yes, I can," Rain said.

"Great. I appreciate it. We'll be gone all next week. Okay?"

"Yup."

Rain bought plastic bags at the hardware store. He dutifully wrapped his customer's papers and put them on the back porch of the house. When he collected the money for the week's papers, the customer was indeed appreciative. "Thank you, Rain, for wrapping my papers. I know it was an extra cost and extra time for you. Here's seven bucks," said the customer.

"Thanks," said a happy Rain.

The next day every paper Rain delivered was wrapped in plastic. On the front page of each paper was a note:

Wrapped by Rain, Your Paperboy.

Rain's tips doubled.

Rain's packaging innovation was soon noticed by *The Gazette*. The plastic wrapping dramatically decreased *The Gazette*'s cost of providing free papers to compensate for papers that got wet or damaged after delivery.

In a few years, it was common practice for newspapers all over the country to deliver plastic-wrapped papers.

CHAPTER 17

COFFEE

R ain discovered something obvious. He "discovered" that most of his customers read *The Gazette* in the morning. He also "discovered" that most of his customers read the paper while drinking coffee. When he returned home from delivering his morning route, his parents would be reading their paper over coffee at the kitchen table. While riding on the morning school bus, Rain saw people sitting at tables and counters, reading *The Gazette* and drinking coffee. He saw commuters at the train station holding the paper in one hand and a coffee cup in the other.

"Coffee and newspaper, newspaper and coffee," Rain thought. "It's like ham and eggs, like shoes and socks. They go together."

An idea began to percolate in Rain's fertile brain.

A few days later, Rain rode his bike to the Coffee Corner. He went inside and asked to speak to the person in charge. A few minutes later, one of the owners, a guy dressed in a black turtleneck, approached Rain. The fellow looked surprised to see it was a kid asking for him. "Hi, I'm Jamie Flaherty. Can I help you?"

"Hi. My name is Rain. I have an idea that I think could bring you more customers."

"Cool. What's your idea?"

"I am a paperboy. I deliver *The Gazette* to fifty-nine houses every single day. My customers like to drink coffee when they read the paper. My idea is that you print up coupons that look something like this." Rain handed Jamie two three- by five-inch pieces of paper.

One read:

> "Welcome to the Coffee Corner.
>
> One Free Muffin with a Cup of Coffee.
>
> A Free Gift from Rain, Your Paperboy."

The other read:

> "Visit the Coffee Corner.
>
> $1.00 Off a Dozen Doughnuts.
>
> A Free Gift from Rain, Your Paperboy."

Jamie was amazed. "Not bad," he said.

"If you think this is a good campaign and are willing to offer my customers these promotions or something similar, I can include coupons like these with my daily papers. I would deliver them free of charge to my entire customer list, so it's great advertising for your business."

"So how will it work?" Jamie asked. "We print them? You deliver them?"

"Right. Whatever it costs you to print a hundred coupons will probably be wiped out by selling a few dozen extra doughnuts or by getting just one or two new steady customers." Rain explained.

"I like it. We do promotions like this all the time. And if you deliver, we won't have to pay postage. But what's in it for you?" Jamie asked.

"I think my customers will thank me for the coupon and will give me more tips," Rain explained.

"Got it." Jamie smiled. "Give me your address. I'll send the coupons as soon as they are printed. Anything else, Rain?"

"Yes. My customers want great muffins and fresh bagels."

"Nothing but the best for your . . . ah, for our, customers, Rain."

CHAPTER 18

ROOKIE

—

"Rain," called Mom, "Mr. D'Michaels of *The Gazette* is on the phone for you."

"Hello," Rain said.

"Hi, Rain, how's it going?" Mr. D'Michaels asked.

"Fine. School ends Friday, and my first Babe Ruth game is Saturday."

"Sounds good. Anyway, I'm calling you for a number of reasons. Do you have a few minutes?"

"Sure."

"First of all, congratulations on completing your first year as a paperboy."

"Thanks."

"You should be proud of yourself. Lots of kids don't last a month, but you said you would make it, and you did. In appreciation, *The Gazette* is giving you a fifty-dollar gift certificate to any store you want," Mr. D'Michaels said. "You can even use it to buy tickets to the Bantams baseball games."

"Fifty bucks! Fantastic! Thank you very much."

"Do you have a favorite store, such as Toys Ahoy?" Mr. D'Michaels asked.

Yeah, so I could, like, buy a little wooden train set, Rain thought. "Can I get it for Sanibels?" he asked aloud.

"Sanibels? Isn't Sanibels a women's store?" Mr. D'Michaels asked.

Duh-uh! Rain thought. "Yes, it is," he politely answered.

"No problem. I have some more good news. Every year *The Gazette* holds a big awards banquet for all our paper delivery people. We would like to invite you and your parents to be our special guests. Here is the big news. You, Rain, have won our Paperboy Rookie of the Year Award. Your Coffee Corner idea, and your crazy bike, and your reliability were all factors in your being chosen. Congratulations again," Mr. D'Michaels said.

Rain said nothing. Mr. D'Michaels listened to silence.

"Rain, you there?" Mr. D'Michaels asked.

"Yeah, sorry. I'm Rookie of the Year?" Rain squeaked.

"Yup, you beat out sixty other kids."

"I'm Rookie of the Year?" Rain repeated.

"You got it."

More silence.

"Hey, Mom," Rain yelled. "I made Rookie of the Year at *The Gazette*!"

Mr. D'Michaels chuckled.

"I can't believe it," Rain said into the phone.

"Believe it, kid. You are Rookie of the Year. And you're gonna get your picture in the paper."

"Hey, Mom," Rain yelled again, "they're gonna put my picture in the paper!"

"So do you think you guys can make the banquet?" Mr. D'Michaels asked.

"I'm sure we can," Rain said while thinking, *I hope I don't have a game that night.*

He then asked, "Mr. D'Michaels, will I get the gift certificate before the banquet?"

"Vern will deliver your gift certificate tomorrow. The banquet will be at the end of the month. Okay?" Mr. D'Michaels asked.

"Okay! Perfect! Thanks again. Thanks for calling. Bye."

"Rain, Rookie of the Year! Wait 'til your father hears. He will be so proud," Mom said.

"And guess what else, Mom," Rain asked.

73

"Okay, Mr. Smiley Face, what else?" Mom beamed.

"I'm buying you something to wear to the awards banquet!"

"That's very nice of you, Rain, but I don't want you spending your hard-earned money on me."

"I'm not," he said. "For finishing my first year, *The Gazette* gave me a fifty-dollar gift certificate to your favorite store, Sanibels. There is nothing in that store I like, so you can have the gift certificate," he proclaimed.

"That is very generous of you. Thank you."

"You're welcome." Running up the stairs, Rain hollered, "Woo-woo! Rookie of the Year!"

Mom laughed at Rain's cheering and thought, *Why on earth would* The Gazette *give a fourteen-year-old boy a gift certificate to a woman's clothing store? Why not to miniature golf or a sports store? Surely they know that boys love . . . that boys love . . . that boys. . . .*

She was still standing at the kitchen sink listening to Rain whoop it up when Rain's father walked in from the garage. "What's the matter?" he asked, "Why are you crying?"

"Rain won Paperboy Rookie of the Year," she whispered.

CHAPTER 19

PHOTO

———

"Is that what you're wearing for your picture today?" Mom asked.

"Yup," answered Rain.

"Rain, I don't know. Mr. D'Michaels is sending out a reporter and a photographer. I'm not sure this is what they have in mind for the article."

"It's fine, Mom. Mr. D'Michaels said I could wear whatever I want, and this is it."

"But, Rain, the article is not going to be in the sports section. It is going to be in Town News."

"Don't worry, Mom. They don't care."

"I'm not worried, Rain. I just think you would look so cute wearing your *Gazette* delivery bag over your shoulder. Something like that. And you could still wear your baseball cap, but push it up so people can see your face."

So cute! Gag me, Rain thought. "Hey, I think they're here," he said.

"Okay," Mom sighed, "but at least lose the base-ball glove. People will think you won Rookie of the Year in the major leagues."

"C'mon, Mom. You gotta have the glove."

Rain flashed out the door and all Mom could see was her "Number 9" running down the walk.

The next day, a few of Rain's customers and friends of his mom and dad called with congratulations. Mom said, "You were right, Rain. Everyone loved the article, especially your photo. Mrs. Christopher said you looked darling in your little baseball suit. She's thrilled you are her paperboy."

Rain thought, *Looked darling in my little base-ball suit! Uniform, ladies, uniform."* The next week, Rain's tips doubled on collection day.

Rain's mother framed the newspaper article and photo (of course) and hung it over Rain's desk. Rain glanced at the photo as he filled out his weekly bank deposit slip. In a reasonably inspired mimicry of base-ball great Roberto Clemente's unforgettable "thank you," Rain said aloud, to himself, "Base-ah-ball has been-ah veddy good to me."

CHAPTER 20

CRIME AND
PUNISHMENT

―――

R ain's mother picked up the ringing phone.
"Hello," she said.

"Hello. This is Frank Driscoll."

"Hi, Frank. How are you?" Mom said.

"I'm fine. But I'm afraid our Rain has gotten himself in trouble."

"Uh-oh. Is it bad?" Rain's mom asked the school principal.

"It's not the end of the world: Rain and two other kids on the baseball team played hooky from school today. They all called in sick, but one of our teachers spotted them getting tickets over at Muzzy Field. I guess it's the Triple-A Minor League series or something."

"So what do you want to do?" Mom asked.

"These are good kids, but rules are rules. I'll need your permission, but what do you think if I made the boys spend three hours each working at Centerfield next Saturday?"

"Centerfield? Is that the retirement place over on Hungerford?" Mom asked.

"Yes. They call it independent living. All the people are retired, but they are a spry group. They have several married couples. The deal is that they live on their own until, or if, they need health care. And Centerfield has excellent health care," Mr. Driscoll said.

"Fine with me. Maybe Rain will learn a lesson working with senior citizens," Mom said.

"And many accomplished and successful seniors," Mr. Driscoll said.

"Thanks, Frank," Mom said.

"Thank you."

When Rain got home, his mother asked if he had a minute.

"What's up, Mom?" Rain asked.

"Who won the game?" Mom asked.

"The game?"

"Yes, the game. You know. The game they play over at Muzzy Field. I think they call it baseball. That game." Mom said.

"Oh. That game," said a subdued Rain.

"Coming back to you? After all you were probably there, what, for six hours or so, and left an hour ago," Mom said.

"Two good games, Mom. Real good," Rain said.

"You broke the rules," Mom admonished.

"Well, Mr. Driscoll called, and you and the other two delinquents are going to spend Saturday morning working over at Centerfield. Centerfield is a retirement community for senior citizens. I'm sure there is a lot of work for you to do there."

"Okay," Rain said.

"All right. Now go do your homework."

The next Saturday, with flags flying, Green Lightning went into a sand-spraying power slide skidding to a stop outside Centerfield's main entrance. It was 7:55 A.M. Rain parked his bike near a strapped bale of *Gazette* papers leaning against a portico column. Rain walked in and approached the woman working at the front desk.

"Hi, I'm Rain. I'm here to work."

"Good morning, Rain. My name is Mrs. Bemis. We were expecting you. Your first job is in the main dining hall. Our residents who use the dining hall have finished breakfast. You can help the staff clean up. When you're done, come back and see me. Okay?"

"Sure. When does breakfast start?" Rain asked.

"Six-thirty for the early risers, which is just about everyone who doesn't take breakfast in their apartment."

"And everyone is gone now?" Rain asked.

"Yes, the residents are already doing different things now. Some are probably already getting ready for today's croquet tournament. Another group went to the casino, others are playing bridge, some are in the exercise class—that kind of thing.

"Okay, how do I get there?" Rain asked.

In about an hour, Rain was back at the front desk. "What's next?" he asked.

"That was fast," said Mrs. Bemis. "Go see Miss Catherine. Catherine is our social director. She knows you're coming. Some of the residents will be in the gathering rooms. Some might be in their apartments. You are going to visit the residents with Catherine. If they need anything, Catherine will have you get what they need, okay?"

"Okay."

"Up the stairs, first station on the right."

"Okay."

Catherine met Rain with a smile. "Rain. You push this cart. It's loaded with books, bottles of water, menus of local restaurants—that type of thing. Ready?"

Ready as Rain, Rain thought to himself. "Ready." he said aloud.

"Good morning, Mrs. Mullen. And how are you this fine morning?" greeted Catherine.

Mrs. Mullen was elegant. She was seated in a high-back chair. She had perfectly coiffed grey-flecked black hair. She wore pearls, obvious earrings, and lipstick. Her dress was dark blue. Her half-glasses, balanced at the end of her nose, were secured with a gold chain.

"The same as yesterday. I woke up. I'm still kickin'. But where is my newspaper? I want to see if I'm in the obituary section," Mrs. Mullen chortled.

"Very funny," Catherine said.

A *real riot*, Rain thought to himself.

"Who are you?" Mrs. Mullen asked.

"I'm Rain."

"What are you doing here with Cathy?"

"I'm helping out today."

"Well, help me out and find my newspaper. I want to read it before it's ancient history."

"Rain," said Catherine, "the papers are probably downstairs somewhere."

"I know where they are. I'll be back in a minute," Rain said as he shot out of the room.

Rain borrowed scissors from Mrs. Bemis and opened the bale of *Gazettes*. He delivered Mrs. Mullen's paper in less than five minutes.

"Thank you, Rain. Now be a good boy and deliver the papers to my friends. Cathy, do you have a list of who gets *The Gazette?*" Mrs. Mullen commanded.

"I'll get the list," Catherine said and left.

"Mrs. Mullen," Rain asked, "when do you usually get your paper?"

"A different time every day. Different people are on duty during the week. I have to ask every day."

"When would you like to get your paper?" Rain asked.

"I want the paper when the day starts. That's when I start. And so does everybody else."

"Is it okay to put the paper in that mail slot, or whatever that is in your front door?"

"Perfectly fine," Mrs. Mullen said.

"Rain, here's the list. Names and room numbers," said Catherine.

"I'm on it," Rain said, and he took off.

Later, Rain said to Mrs. Bemis, "The residents want their morning paper delivered to their apartments before breakfast."

"I know, I know," said Mrs. Bemis. "But the papers come early, and we usually don't have someone available to bring them in and get them to the residents."

"May I use your phone? I think I have an answer."

"By all means. Here's the phone," said Mrs. Bemis.

Raid called Vern.

"Hi, Vern. This is Rain. I'm over at the Centerfield."

Rain listened. "Yeah, the fancy place. You ought to see their workout room. It's got everything.

"Vern, the problem is that someone delivers *The Gazette* in the morning but just leaves the bale outside and there's no system to get the papers delivered to the apartments in the complex."

Rain listened. "By breakfast time. These people have breakfast before the birds get up, and everyone who works here is too busy to get the papers."

Rain listened. "What's a corporate account?"

Vern talked for a minute.

"Okay," responded Rain, "how about this? You have someone drop off the bale. I'll deliver the papers to the customers. The Centerfield still pays *The Gazette* for all the papers, and you pay me the regular ten cents per paper." Rain asked.

Rain listened. "I'll bet when I start delivering, we will get those people back."

Rain listened. "Mrs. Bemis said they're always complaining. And there is a Mrs. Mullen here. She's like a queen or something. She's for it."

He listened some more and said, "Okay, thanks Vern. I'll tell 'em. Bye."

Then Rain turned to Mrs. Bemis: "Okay, Mrs. Bemis. Starting Monday, it'll be papers with pancakes."

"Thank you, Rain. You don't know how many people here will be grateful. I shouldn't say this, but I'm happy you skipped school the other day."

"Me, too, Mrs. Bemis. Me, too!"

Riding his bike home, Rain did the math in his head. *Twenty papers a day, six days: 120 papers at ten cents is a fast twelve dollars a week, not including the Sundays. Tips or no tips. Not bad, my man, not bad.*

Later that afternoon, Mom said to Rain, "Well I hope you learned your lesson this morning."

Try twelve bucks a week, Rain thought.

"Sure did, Mom."

"Good."

CHAPTER 21

COLLECTIONS

———

Most of Rain's customers were nice: most paid him every week, and most gave him a tip every week. Sometimes people weren't home when Rain visited to collect the money for the week's papers, and sometimes he had to collect for two or three weeks of papers, but the customers always paid. Except one.

One house was a problem for Rain. Rain called it the "politics house" because the front yard was always full of signs saying, "Vote for this guy," or "Don't vote for that guy," or "Vote yes, or no, on some kind of proposition." Rain didn't care one iota about politics: he had more important things to do. The house was owned by a man and his wife who, Rain figured, were older than his parents. Neither person was nice. They never said hello. They insisted that Rain put their morning paper between the front storm door and the entrance door.

They warned Rain to close the door quietly so as not to wake them. Neither ever thanked Rain.

And they never gave him a tip, they rarely paid on time, and they were hard to collect from. When Rain went to collect, if the man answered the door, he would tell Rain to come back when his wife was home. The man told Rain that his wife paid "delivery people." If the wife answered the door, she would tell Rain that her husband had to review all bills before paying, or that she had just paid the gardener, or whatever, and Rain would have to come back. When they did pay, they always questioned the bill.

This time the "politics house" had not paid in eight weeks. Because they received the paper seven days a week, they owed Rain eight times $2.50 a week, or $20.00. Because Rain paid *The Gazette* for all the papers he delivered, the politics house was putting him in a hole. Once or twice a week, Rain attached to the front page of the politics house newspaper an envelope with his name on it and a polite note that said, "Reminder: your newspaper bill is now $7.50 [or $10.00 or $15.00]." But he still didn't get paid.

Vern suggested that Rain leave a note saying, "Paper delivery might be interrupted due to unpaid bill." Rain left the note. After three more deliveries, he still was not paid.

At dinner, Rain's parents discussed the upcoming presidential election. Rain knew that every four years, people voted for a new president, but that's all he knew. The baseball season was over; soccer and hockey had started. That's what mattered.

"This is the closest election in years," Rain heard his father say. "All the television networks are making predictions, and all the newspapers are endorsing their candidates. The political junkies are going crazy."

"Dad," Rain asked, "when is the election?"

"Next Tuesday, November 8."

Wednesday morning, November 9, was a typical November stormy day in New England. It was raining, and raining hard. Leaves were blowing everywhere. In his raincoat, Rain stood next to Green Lightning, his bike, flashing in the driveway of the politics house, with political signs bucking and shaking all around him. The porch light went on just before 6:00 A.M. The front door opened, and the man eagerly reached down for his paper. Instead of the paper, there was just an envelope, with "Rain: Your Paperboy," neatly printed across the front. The man's head jerked up. He saw Rain in the driveway and wildly waved for Rain to approach the house. Rain didn't move. The man called out to Rain and, in vain, waved again. Minutes later, in bathrobe and boots, struggling to control an umbrella, the man shuffled down the driveway to where Rain stood, holding his flashing bike.

"What's the matter? What's going on? Where is our paper?" the man demanded.

"I have it right here, sir," Vern said, approaching from his truck. "I work for *The Gazette*. Rain told us there was a problem with your unpaid bill. We are concerned that you are dissatisfied with our delivery service or have a problem with your paperboy. Is there a problem?"

"Uh, no. No. No. There's no problem. No."

Vern said nothing. Rain watched.

"No. There's no problem. Did my wife forget to pay? What do we owe? No problem. The kid can come by this afternoon, and we'll take care of it."

Vern said nothing.

The wind and the rain and the leaves and the "Vote for Dufus" signs were all that moved.

The man looked at Vern. "How much do we owe?" he asked.

"Twenty-two fifty. Twenty bucks late and $2.50 for this week," Rain said.

"Okay. Just a minute. Wait here."

The man trundled back to the house, then returned and handed Rain twenty-three dollars and said, "Keep the change."

"Thank you," Rain said.

The man mumbled something, then looked expectantly at Vern.

Newspaper in hand, Vern said, "Okay. You don't have any problems. That's good. Let me ask you one more thing: Will Rain have any problems?"

The man stared at Vern. Vern said nothing.

"No problems," the man said. Vern handed him the paper. The guy walked back to his house.

Rain turned to Vern. "Thank you, Vern."

"You are completely welcome," Vern said.

"Hey, Vern, who won the election?" Rain asked.

"You did, kid. You did."

CHAPTER 22

ICE

A brook about fifteen feet wide and two feet deep cut through Rain's territory. There was no footbridge, so in the summer, Rain had to ride his bike on the road, which crossed over the brook. Sometimes in the winter, when the weather was consistently below freezing, the brook would freeze over. The brook waters generally flowed crisply, although the brook would freeze, in some places the ice was five inches thick and in others just an inch or so. Rain liked it when the brook froze over. Instead of using the road, he could cross the brook on a fallen tree frozen into the ice and save a lot of time. Rain had ten customers who lived on the other side of the brook. Although he had to park his bike and then walk across the brook, the shortcut saved ten or fifteen minutes.

Crossing the tree was a balancing act. Rain would load one of his bags with ten papers and then nimbly, carefully, gingerly he would tightrope across the frozen brook.

Rain liked delivering his last ten papers because it meant his route was over. After his last paper, he could go home, eat breakfast, get his book bag, and catch the school bus. On this day, more than usual, Rain was looking forward to the last ten deliveries. For on this day, it was bitterly cold, maybe only ten degrees, and light snow was falling. Rain wanted to finish his route, go home, and drink his mom's hot chocolate.

With his paper bag slung over his back, Rain started to cross the brook. Halfway over, his foot slipped off the log, but the ice was firm, and Rain bounded up the bank into the neighborhood. It was still snowing. To keep warm and finish quickly, Rain jogged and speed-walked through his route.

Finished, Rain ran back to his bridge. He took two steps and abruptly fell sideways off the snow-slicked tree trunk. He crashed through the ice and went completely under the water. His knees and hands touched the bottom. He bolted up. He was standing. The water was knee deep. He plunged through the water to the edge of the solid ice. He tried to climb the ice but there was nothing to grab. The ice was too slippery. The bag for his papers was full of water, and the weight of it pulled him backward. He fell again. His butt hit the bottom of the brook. Ice cold water rushed into his mouth and down inside his coat. Gagging, Rain stood up again.

It's not over my head, Rain flashed. *I can touch.*

He grabbed a branch of the fallen tree and pulled himself onto the tree, then belly-crawled and knee-crawled to his bike. Rain's hat was soaked. His mittens were soaked. His boots were full of water. Rain's clothes were so wet, so heavy he could not pick up his bike. It was deadly cold. Rain dropped his bag on Green Lightning and started running home. His jacket and pants started to freeze. His face numbed. His nostrils burned with every breath. His ears were on fire. Rain's boots weighed a million pounds.

His feet were leaden. Rain did not stop running. Down the street, he could see that his kitchen lights were on. Rain ran and crashed through his back door.

Rain's mom was in the kitchen. She gasped when she saw Rain She darted to help him remove his clothes. She couldn't do much. Rain's hat was frozen to his head. His jacket zipper was frozen. She turned on the shower and pushed him into it fully clothed. In minutes, Rain was shedding his clothes and getting warm.

Later, warmly dressed, sipping Mom's hot chocolate, eating toast with jelly, Rain thought how lucky he was. He had had a close call. He thought he was lucky because he had fallen into the brook *after* he had delivered his last ten papers. If he had fallen in on the way to his customers, he would have lost ten papers, lost ten sales, lost money, maybe lost his life or gotten a frostbitten ear.

"Rain," he said aloud to himself, "you are one lucky paperboy."

CHAPTER 23

EXIT STRATEGY

"Vern," Rain said, "I'm gonna have to give up the route."

"Yup," Vern said.

"I don't have the time. I have practice every day after school, and I have tons of homework."

"Yup."

"My route is so much bigger. I'm playing American Legion and Park Department this summer. I could probably do the route this summer, but definitely not after school starts."

"I figured," Vern said.

"What do I do?"

"The kid before you just up and quit. No notice. We scrambled to deliver the papers until you took over. We don't want to go through that again."

"So what do I do?" Rain asked.

"Sell it," Vern answered.

"Sell what? Sell the paper route?"

"Yup."

"I can do that? I can sell the paper route, what, to some other kid?"

"Yup," Vern said. "Although we'll have to approve the new kid."

"So I find a kid and sell him the paper route? I give him a price, and he gives me the money? You say okay, and he takes over? Is that right?"

"Yup," Vern said.

"Does *The Gazette* get any of the money?"

"Nope. They'd rather have you find and train a new kid than do it themselves. D'Michaels will be for it. We've done it before. I did it myself a hundred years ago. As they say, it's a win-win."

"Okay," said Rain. "School is over in a month. I'll find someone to buy my route. I can train him in June."

Rain let the word out that he was selling his route. After talking to several kids, Rain found the perfect replacement. Mr. D'Michaels and Vern both liked the kid. The only thing left to do was to sell the route.

CHAPTER 24

VALUATION

——

"Dad, I have a kid who wants to buy the route, but a lot depends on the price. I didn't give a price yet, because I'm not sure. How do I figure it out?"

"Sometimes selling something is more than just the price," Dad explained. "Even if something has a fair price, if the buyer doesn't have the money or can't get the money, then there might be no sale. Does this kid have any money?"

"I don't know. Probably. Maybe the parents. Why talk about buying something if you don't have money?" Rain asked.

"True. All right, first let's figure out what your route is worth. Then you can figure a sale price later."

"All right," Rain said.

"Okay. How many Monday through Saturday customers do you have?"

"Eighty-two, counting twenty at Centerfield," Rain answered.

"And you make ten cents a paper, correct?"

"Correct."

"So that's 82 times 10 cents times 6 days. Let's see. That's $49.20 a week you make, right?"

"Right," Rain said.

"Times fifty-two weeks."

"I take off two weeks in August," Rain reminded him.

"That's okay. We'll use fifty-two weeks because that gives the total profit. The new kid may not take any days off."

"Right. Could be," Rain agreed.

"So 52 times $49.20, make it $49, is $2,548 a year. Round off to $2,550. Okay?"

"Plus the Sundays," Rain said.

"How many Sunday papers do you have, and what do you make per paper?"

"Seventy Sundays at 25 cents a pop," Rain answered.

"That's 70 times 25 cents, which is $17.50 a week. That's $910 a year," Dad calculated. "We add $2,550 for the daily papers, plus $910 for the Sundays, gives $3,460 income for the year. That's good," Dad said.

"Dad. I think we need to cut that a bit. There are probably ten or so customers who stop the paper for vacations and stuff. And about five of the Centerfielders go to Florida or France or someplace."

"Very good, Rain. That is important and honest. A new paperboy would probably not think of that. There's an old expression, 'The buyer needs a thousand eyes; the seller needs but one.' But I think looking out for the buyer is good business," Dad said.

"Yeah," Rain said. "So ten customers leave for two weeks, or fourteen days. One customer is worth 6 times 10 cents plus 25 cents on Sunday, or 85 cents a week. So I lose 10 customers times 85 cents times 2 weeks. That's $17, right?"

"Right. I thought it would be more than that," Dad said.

"It's higher if you do it on sales. Each customer pays $2.50 a week, but I get only 85 cents. The rest goes to *The Gazette*."

"What about Centerfield?" Dad asked.

"Let's say five customers take off for fifty days each. That's close. Fifty days is like seven full weeks. So 5 customers times 7 weeks times $.85 a week is about $35," Rain figured aloud.

"So we have $17 plus $35, or $52. Want to say $60 to be safe?" Dad asked.

"More than safe," Rain answered.

"Okay, your total income is $3,460 minus $60, or $3,400. Right?" Dad asked.

"Yes, right," Rain said. "What about tips?"

"We have to add them. What do you estimate your tips are on a weekly basis, or whatever?" Dad asked.

"Last year I got $250 from the Centerfielders for Christmas. Mrs. Mullen said she had everyone chip in."

"Yes, I do recall your screaming. And everyone got a thank-you note, I presume?" Dad asked.

"You presume right," Rain quipped.

"You were saying," Dad prodded.

"I got $250 from the Centerfielders, and on average, about $30 to $40 a week during the year from the regular customers, and about $500 at Christmas. What's that?" Rain asked.

"It's $250 plus $500 plus 50 weeks, because you take two weeks off, times $30. Okay?" Dad asked.

"Right."

"That's $750 plus $1,500, so $2,250 in total tips. Add that to $3,400, and you hauled in $5,650."

And I am worth every penny, Rain thought to himself.

Rain said nothing.

"What about expenses?" Dad asked.

"Not too much. We're not counting the two weeks money I give my sub in August. I get some flats, so two new tires a year. Maybe forty, fifty bucks. New lights and streamers for Green Lightning. Dog treats. This and that. Say a hundred bucks, two hundred max, max, max," Rain answered.

"That's good. Most businesses have all kinds of costs and expenses, such as gas, lights, rent, and such they have to pay. Your biggest cost is your labor, which you pay to yourself. If we deduct $200, that means your route made you around $5,450.

The route *made me $5,450?* Rain thought. *Un-uh Daddy-O, El Raino made the money, not the route.*

Rain said nothing.

"Here's how the money adds up," Dad said, handing Rain a note pad.

"Looks good to me," Rain said.

"One of the variables in all this," Dad said, "is your tip money. Do you think the other kid can get what you get?"

Without my smile, it'll take a while, Rain wisecracked to himself. He said aloud, "Probably. The people are nice, but I don't know."

"Consider that when setting your price," Dad said.

"What about the paper raising prices? Vern told me they're probably going up. This means making more money per paper," Rain said.

"Good point. A good selling point. But I don't think we should try to put a number on it," Dad advised.

"Dad," Rain asked, "what's a good selling price?"

"This is tricky. Companies and people buy existing companies all the time. There are all kinds of factors that go into valuating a company, determining what a company is worth. In some industries, buyers use rules of thumbs," Dad explained.

"One more thing. I think the new kid should get more for delivering the Sundays. It should be at least forty cents, not twenty-five. I might mention that to Mr. D'Michaels."

"Another good selling point," Dad said.

Dad continued explaining: "Some companies might set a purchase price, or selling price, at, say, three times net profit, or four times, or some number. If that were the case for paper routes, your route would be worth $15,000 to $20,000."

"No way!" Rain exclaimed.

"Exactly right, Rain. No way. That's because a company buying a paper route would have to hire a paper-boy, or delivery person, and pay that person by the hour, or by the week, or something. If they bought your route as a business, they might have to pay someone two to three thousand dollars a year to deliver the papers. And the buying company would not get any tips. The paperboy would. So to a company, a paper route is not worth much. This is why newspapers don't employ full-time paperboys. They wouldn't make enough money. You with me?"

"Kind of," Rain answered.

"Look at it this way. You made $5,450. But you worked, what, two hours a day?" Dad asked.

"More or less," Rain answered.

"Two hours a day times 350 days is 700 hours. Divide $5,450 by 700, and you earned about $7 plus change an hour. But the real number for an adult or someone with a family is the $14 or $15 a day you make. Pretty much, only a kid living at home can afford to work for $15 a day."

"So what price would you set?" Rain asked.

"You want to sell it, right? You no longer want to work for $15 a day. The lower the price, the easier it is to sell. You'll have to think about it."

Rain was always thinking. "Dad, how about this? Will you or Mom type up the math you did? I give the numbers to the new kid to look over. Then we make a deal."

"I'll ask Mom. She is a much better typist than I am," Dad said.

A short time later, Mom finished typing Rain's and his father's calculations.

"Rain," Mom said, "the business numbers are impressive. But I do have a concern. I remember that P.J. quit because the job was probably too tough. And I remember how hard it was for you in the beginning and how hard it is to get up so early. And I remember your falling in the frozen brook. This worries me."

Rain said nothing.

"What if the job is too hard? What if the paperboy gets sick, or the parents have to move? The paperboy pays you something for the route and can't work long enough to get his money back. That bothers me," Mom said.

Rain nodded, and said nothing.

The next day Rain brought his business numbers to school.

Rain's Route Revenue

Daily paper selling price	$.25
Daily paper net money to paperboy	$.10
Sunday paper selling price	$1.00
Sunday paper net money to paperboy	$.25
Daily customers	82
Sunday customers	70

Daily papers income to paperboy:
82 papers × .$10 a paper × 6 days
× 52 weeks = $2,558.40

Rounded to $2,550

Sunday paper income to paperboy:
70 papers × $.25 a paper times
52 weeks = $910

TOTAL paper income = $3,460, rounded
to $3,400

Weekly tip income: $30 (minimum per
week) × 50 weeks = $1,500

Christmas tips = $500

Centerfield tip =	$250
Tips income =	$2,250
Paper income =	$3,400
Total income =	$5,650

Deductions and Expenses

Lost income due to customer vacations =	$60
Expenses for bike tires, dog treats, upkeep	$200
Total expenses =	$260
Net annual profit to paperboy =	$5,390—5,450
Average =	$5,400

CHAPTER 25

NEGOTIATION

———

R ain and the new kid met at Pops's diner.

"Hi, Pops. Hi, Mrs. Pops," Rain said.

"Good morning, Rain. Counter or table?" Mrs. Pops asked.

"A table, please," Rain answered.

"Just going to be the two of you?" Mrs. Pops asked.

"Just us."

"Let's go over to your regular table," Mrs. Pops said as she winked at Rain.

"Would you like something to eat or drink?" Mrs. Pops asked.

"A Coke, please."

"A Pepsi for me, thank you."

As Mrs. Pops walked away, the new kid marveled, "Your regular table? Have you done, like, business here before?"

"Yes. I have."

"Cool."

"Did you go over the facts and figures I gave you," asked Rain.

"Yup, they're right here. I went over them with my father. He was surprised at how much money you are making. He believes the numbers, though, because my parents know your parents."

Mrs. Pops delivered the two sodas.

"Thank you."

"Thank you."

"You're welcome."

"What do you think the route is worth?" Rain asked.

"I'm not sure. I don't know if I can get the tips and extras you get. What do you want for the route?"

"I'm looking for $1,700. That's half the money you keep after paying for the papers, not counting tips," Rain said.

"Whew. That's a lot of money. I'm not sure my parents will lend me that much."

Rain sipped his soda. He said nothing.

"How about $500?" the new kid asked.

"Five hundred? Not counting tips, you will make about $70 a week. In ten weeks, you will make $700. Five hundred is too cheap," Rain replied.

106

The new kid said nothing.

Rain sipped his soda. Rain waited.

"Do you think I can earn a lot in tips?"

"Definitely," Rain said. "The people are really nice."

"I don't know," the new kid said.

Rain said nothing.

"I'm worried I might not make it. I want the job, but what if I can't do it?"

"I think you can do it. But are you worried that if you pay a lot of money and then something happens, you will have lost your money?"

"That's it," the new kid answered.

"Okay. How about this? You pay me one hundred dollars to start. If you make it two months, eight weeks, you pay me another three hundred. Then at your twenty-fifth week, you pay me the final four hundred bucks. That's a total of eight hundred dollars. You will have made at least seventeen hundred plus tips. So you will easily be able to pay. How does that sound?"

The new kid studied the paper with the business numbers.

Rain waited.

"All I'm really risking is a hundred dollars?"

Rain nodded.

"I think my parents would be okay with this."

Rain said nothing.

"All right," the new kid said. "I'll buy it."

"Do we have a deal?" Rain asked.

"Deal!" the new kid said.

They shook hands.

Rain said, "I'll write it up on this napkin. You sign. I'll sign. And Mrs. Pops can sign as a witness. Okay?"

"Fine."

Signing the napkin, Mrs. Pops asked, "Still doing business deals, Rain?"

"Yup," Rain said.

"Two more sodas?" Mrs. Pops asked.

"Yes, please," Rain said. "And I'm buying."

"Good," the new kid said. "You just cleaned me out."

Everyone laughed.

CHAPTER 26

THE NEW KID

Rain and the new kid met for their first training trip.

"First, I'm going to take you on a complete tour of the route. Then I'm going to introduce you to some of my nicest customers. Later I will introduce you to all of my, I mean, your customers. And I will tell you all about the dogs in the neighborhood. The Centerfielders. Wellington Heights. Everything. How does that sound?" asked Rain.

"Perfect," the new kid said.

"Okay, let's roll."

"My parents are the best," Rain said, "but they kind of don't count. Mr. and Mrs. Burrows are wicked nice. We'll meet them first, okay?"

"Okay," the new kid said.

"Hi, Mrs. Burrows. This is the new kid who's taking over my route. You will get great service."

"Hello to you, Rain. And who might you be?" Mrs. Burrows asked.

"I am Brenna Rose O'Brien. I am in the eighth grade at Towpath. I play soccer, not," she glanced at Rain, "baseball. I am your new papergirl."

"Delighted," Mrs. Burrows said, extending her hand. "And I love your braids and your pink high-top sneakers."

"Thank you."

Rain and Brenna Rose pedaled their bikes down the street.

"She is nice," Brenna Rose said.

"Just like I told you."

"Hey, Rain?"

"Yeah," Rain replied.

"How much you want for Green Lightning?"

CHAPTER 27

THE BULLY
(PART II)

R ain was no longer a paperboy. He had sold his
route to Brenna Rose O'Brien. Now he was a
sophomore in high school, and Chuckie was a senior.
Both boys had grown, and Rain was now the same
height as Chuckie. Both boys were on their school's var-
sity basketball team. Chuckie was a starter, and Rain
was a sub. The team had an away game. As usual before
an away game, the players drifted into the locker room,
hung around the school, and then boarded the bus for
the trip to the opposing team's town.

Whereas Rain was always early for everything,
Chuckie was never on time for anything. Game day was
no exception. The team was already on the bus. As
Coach started to board, Chuckie's car came speeding

into the parking lot. Slamming the car door shut, Chuckie rushed to the locker room and flippantly yelled, "Don't leave without me. It'll take a second to get my stuff."

"C'mon, Moriarty! Move it! We've gotta roll," Coach hollered.

Chuckie flew into the school and hurriedly unlocked his locker. His locker was a total mess. Towels and sweatshirts and socks and kneepads tumbled everywhere as Chuckie randomly jammed stuff into his duffle bag.

Two hours later in the visiting team locker room, Chuckie suddenly started shouting, "Which one of you jerks stole my sneakers?

The players looked at Chuckie in bewilderment.

Charlie ratcheted up his rant. "One of you losers stole one of my sneakers. And one of you is gonna pay. And one of you is gonna pay big. And one of you is gonna give me your sneakers for this game."

The locker room was silent.

Chuckie glowered at his teammates. He looked from one player to another. He came to Rain, who stared back.

"What are you looking at?" Chuckie challenged.

Rain said nothing.

"You think this is funny? Well, do you?"

"A little bit," Rain answered.

"Well, now your sneakers are mine. Hand 'em over. Now!"

No one in the locker room moved.

Rain spoke quietly. "If you did pack both your sneakers, what did someone do? Steal one of them out of your duffel bag while it was on the seat next to you?"

Chuckie looked at Rain, then looked around the locker room. He saw the sly smiles and elbow nudges.

Chuckie turned back to Rain. He held out his hand. "I'm starting the game. I'm a senior. You're a sub and a sophomore. Sneakers. Don't make me ask you again!"

Rain said nothing.

"I'm waiting," Chuckie growled.

"Waiting for what?" Rain answered.

Chuckie hesitated. Obviously Rain was no longer a little kid he could push around. "Don't mess with me Rain," Chuckie said.

"One. No one stole your stupid sneakers. No one wants to touch any of your stuff. Two. I'll bet you $142.40 your stupid sneakers are still in your locker back at school. And, three . . . you . . . are . . . not . . . getting . . . my . . . sneakers."

Chuckie's eyes narrowed. The players waited to see Chuckie's next move.

Rain stood. He tensed.

Chuckie hesitated. "I'm gonna tell Coach."

"You're gonna tell me what?" Coach asked.

The kids turned to see Coach standing in the doorway.

How long has he been listening? Rain wondered.

"My sneakers are missing, and Rain is my size, and this is a big game, and if I have his sneakers, I can play and he said he won't give me his sneakers and. . . ."

"Whoa, Chuckie. Take a breath," Coach interrupted. Then he asked, "Was your locker locked?"

"Yeah, the key's in my pants," Chuckie answered.

That's why it's called a locker, Rain quipped to himself.

Coach nodded. "Okay. I understand."

He turned to Rain. "Rain. Chuckie is a starter. Without your sneakers, he can't play."

Rain said nothing.

Coach stared at Rain. "This is a big game. You've always been a team player. Will you give Chuckie your game shoes?"

"No."

"I'm going to ask you, for the team, one more time. Will you please lend Chuckie your shoes?"

"Nope."

Coach looked at Rain. He looked at Rain's implacable face, at Rain's unblinking eyes.

Coach nodded. "Okay, Rain, you're starting tonight. Moriarty, if you want to play tonight, you better find some shoes. Okay, everyone. Out to the court for warm-ups."

Coach walked out of the locker room, and once out of sight from his players, he shook his head, smiled, and thought, *I like that kind of stubborn stand-up in a kid.*

Rain played great that day and started every other game until he graduated. Chuckie never started another game. And he never bothered Rain again.

Three years later, Rain went to college on an academic-athletic scholarship.

Years later, the high school reunion records listed Chuckie Moriarty as "whereabouts unknown."

Mom was right about Chuckie. Moms are always right.

CHAPTER 28

VERN

—

"Mom, Dad, I'm home," called out Rain, closing the front door behind him. He tossed his travel bag in the hallway and went to greet his parents.

"Welcome home," Mom said as she hugged Rain.

"How were your exams?" Dad asked.

"Brutal. But I think I did okay."

"I'm sure you did just fine," Mom said.

"Rain," Dad said, "I'm afraid we have some bad news."

"What do you mean?"

"You remember Mr. D'Michaels of *The Gazette*? Well, he called here a few days ago asking for you. Mom told him you were taking your finals, that you'd probably get home today."

Rain looked at his father. "And?" Rain asked.

"Vern died."

Rain stood still. "What happened?"

"He died over a week ago. After he retired from *The Gazette,* he moved to a retirement home. According to Mr. D'Michaels and his obituary, he died after a short illness. Mr. D'Michaels sent us a copy of Vern's obituary. Here it is."

Rain sat down at the kitchen table and read Vern's obituary. After a moment, he took a deep breath, then another, to keep in control.

"A Silver Star and two Purple Hearts. I never knew that. Vern never said a word."

"Most heroes don't," Dad said.

Rain finished the obituary. "I'm going to save this," he said.

"There's something else," Dad said.

Rain looked up.

"Mr. D'Michaels sent this note and box. They're from Vern to you."

Rain took the note. There was no envelope. Rain looked at the small unwrapped box.

"I think you may want to read that in your room," Mom said. "I have to start dinner. I'm sure you're sick of college food."

Upstairs in his room, Rain smiled as he noticed the "Rookie" story that his mother had framed and proudly hung above his desk. He unfolded Vern's note.

117

Dear Rain:

I hear you are doing well in college. I am not surprised. You've always had the goods.

If you want it, I would like you to have the watch The Gazette gave me some years ago. It keeps perfect time, but I really don't need it anymore. I had a jeweler add something to the back. It's kind of small, but it's big to me.

Your parents are very proud of you, and so am I. Study hard.

> *Your Gazette Colleague,*
> *Vern*

Rain reached for the small box. He fumbled opening it. He got it open. Vern's gold watch was ticking, and the time was correct.

Rain slowly turned over the watch, and read the inscription engraved on the back:

> *To Vern*
> *Our Rainmaker*
> *Your Gazette Friends*

Rain noticed that just beneath "Vern," in tiny letters, there was a new inscription.

To Vern
and Rain
Our Rainmakers
Your Gazette Friends.

Rain fastened Vern's watch to his wrist. It fit perfectly. Rain admired the watch.

"Thank you, Vern. Thanks for everything," Rain said aloud.

A *hero's watch*, he thought.

"Ellis was right: I was born under a lucky star."

CHAPTER 29

GETTING AN M.B.A.

(TWELVE YEARS AFTER RAIN DELIVERED HIS FIRST PAPER)

Rain was having breakfast with his parents.

"How are your applications to business school going?" Dad asked.

"The essays are a bear," Rain answered. "Each school requires several essays, and all are slightly different. My problem is that I want to be different from the other twenty thousand people applying."

"Did you finally decide to which schools you are applying?" Mom asked.

"Wharton, Stanford, Kellogg, Sloan, Fuqua, Columbia, and, of course, Harvard Business School," Rain said.

"Your essays will have to be superb," Dad said.

"Got any ideas?"

"Well, you could write about your three years in the military. Leadership. Achieving the mission. That kind of thing," Dad suggested.

"Why don't you tell them what you learned when you were in Towpath School delivering papers?" Mom suggested.

"As a paperboy? Everyone else is going to talk about their work experience after college. Some guys have worked four or five years in banks, in corporations, in family businesses. How can a kid's paper route compare to that?" Rain asked.

"Rain, your mother is right. It's a great idea. You want to be different, right? Okay, be different. No one else will write about being a paperboy. They will be too conservative. And, who knows? The dean of admissions may be an ex-paperboy. I say go for it," Dad said.

"I'm game," Rain said.

"Why don't you first make a list of the business lessons you learned. Then you can write your essays. Okay?" Dad suggested.

"Well, I learned that forecasting does not mean predicting the weather."

Dad smiled. "Correct. And if you think back, you learned about making money, customer service, sales, and so on. Spend today working on your list. We can go over it tonight."

"We'll be having dinner around seven," Mom said.

Rain instinctively looked at his watch, Vern's watch.

That evening, Rain had his "business lessons learned" list.

"Mom and Dad, I have my list. Do you want to hear what I've got?"

"Of course," Dad said.

"Let's listen after dinner. I don't want your food to get cold," Mom said.

"Okay, after dinner," Dad said.

After clearing the dinner table, Rain announced, "Okay, listen up everybody. Here's what I learned about business when I was a paperboy.

"I think the most important lesson was that the people who buy the paper and pay for it are customers. Without customers, there is no money—no tips, no route to sell, no bank account.

"I also learned a lot about money and pricing and profits. That kind of thing. For example, the paper's price minus what I had to pay *The Gazette* was gross profit. Add the tips and deduct all my other costs gives total net profits. What customers owed me is accounts receivable. What I owed *The Gazette* is accounts payable."

"It amazed me how much money you made in tips," Dad said.

"Well, it didn't amaze me," Mom said. "You were always polite, and you have a friendly smile."

"Good point," Dad said. "Service with smile earns more than service with a shrug."

"Good manners is good business," Mom said. "And courtesy costs nothing."

"Think of all the people who really need tips to live on: waiters and cab drivers and bartenders. Working for tips teaches a lot about tippers and the workers," Rain said.

"I did a lot of things that fall under marketing and advertising. I handed out flyers, asked customers for referrals, did the coupon deal with the Coffee Corner."

"And that coffee idea is called cobranding," Dad said.

"Right. My customers loved that. I also gave free samples of the paper. Customers love to get stuff for free. Lighting my bike was like a moving billboard."

Mom interrupted, "You know, that bike is still in the garage. I wonder if it still works? That was one fancy bike."

"Mom," Rain said, "Green Lightning was the coolest bike on the planet."

"You did market research as well, didn't you?" Dad prompted.

"Yup. My first research was when I was planning to get the job. I talked to some of the neighbors. I think the coin changer idea is what clinched Mr. D'Michaels. And it was market research, in a way, that gave me the idea to sell papers at Pops's Diner. That won me the contest."

"'Won me'?" Mom repeated, raising an eyebrow.

"I mean that's how I won the contest," Rain replied.

"That's better," Mom said.

The Rookie of the Year story in *The Gazette* was good PR," Rain said.

"Everyone loved your picture," Mom said. "With your baseball uniform and *The Gazette* bag. I just wished you had pushed your cap up a bit."

"Mom. That was twelve years ago," Rain said.

"Next time, cap up," Mom said.

"Wrapping the newspaper in plastic was a customer's idea. But after I did it, everyone did it. *The Gazette* saved a lot of money by not having to replace weather-damaged papers."

"That's called investing in quality improvement," Dad said.

"Rain, besides us, of course, who were your best customers?" Mom asked.

"I don't know about best. Mrs. Mullen at the Centerfields was awesome. She made me read *Old Man and the Sea*. She wanted to teach me to play bridge with her crowd, but no time. And she organized the Centerfield tip. Those crazy political people were the worst, but they got better after Vern showed up."

"Speaking of Vern. Guys like that are rare. You learn a lot about getting things done with that kind of man," Dad said.

"He was the best," Rain agreed.

"What else?" Dad asked.

"Lot's of little stuff, like putting the damage discount note on the Sunday papers I wrecked. And the note with my telephone number. And other notes and thank-yous."

"Those little things were big things because everyone remembers your notes," Mom added.

"What was your biggest challenge?" Dad asked.

"After getting my bike legs so I could actually pedal the route, it was the dogs. Some of them were really nasty. I wonder if that one dog ever bit anyone. He was a killer. The guy never figured out that his stupid dog was ripping the papers to get at the raw hamburger."

"What would you have done if he did catch you?" Mom asked.

"Simple. I would give him his paper. I put the hamburger in a day-old paper. It was good for the customer because if he didn't put that dog in the house, I wasn't delivering. Neither would Vern. So he'd have to go and buy the paper someplace."

"Hiring a good sub for our summer vacation was hard."

"That reminds me, "Mom said, "whatever happened to that Chuckie Moriarty?"

"I have no idea where he is, but we evened things out," Rain answered.

"And other challenges?" Dad asked.

"I would have thought falling in the brook in February would rank up there on the challenge list," Mom said. "When you came into the kitchen you looked like a winter carnival ice sculpture."

"It wasn't that bad," Rain smiled. "What was bad was trying to cross the brook on a log. That was dumb."

"Shortcuts are often dumb," Dad said.

"For sure," Rain answered. "I also learned a lot selling the route. Dad helped me figure out the value. Mom, you gave me some good ideas on what the other kid might be thinking. I think it was a fair deal all around. And she paid the whole amount, and paid off early."

"Brenna Rose was a good papergirl," Dad said.

"And as cute as a button," Mom added.

"She was okay," Rain admitted.

"One more thing. I'm grateful that you guys wouldn't let me quit after one day. After getting through those first few days, lots of things were easier. During those two-a-day baseball practices in August, even basic training in the military, I would remember how brutal the paper route was those first few weeks. If I could do the route at thirteen, I could do tougher tasks at any age."

"You are welcome," Dad said. "Your mother and I were dying that week."

You were dying! I was delivering! Rain thought.

"Well, that's it," Rain said aloud.

"But you left out one of the most important lessons," Mom said. "You left out yourself. You left out Rain. You were not called 'paperboy.' Your customers knew you as 'Rain.' 'Rain' was like Gazette or Pampers or Skippy Peanut Butter. What do you call that?"

"A brand name," said Dad. "You are absolutely right."

Pampers? Skippy Peanut Butter? Mom may be right, Rain thought.

"See, Rain, you are a brand, a household name. Mrs. Speath still raves about her cute little paperboy Rain," Mom gushed.

Cute little paperboy! Geez, Mom never changes, Rain thought.

"My opinion," Dad said, "is that what you learned when you were a paperboy was the equivalent of an M.B.A."

"Okay, happy campers, who wants some lemon meringue pie," Mom asked.

"I'm game," Dad said.

"I'm game," Rain said.

Just then the doorbell rang.

"Was that the doorbell?" Dad asked.

"That must be Brenna Rose," Mom said coyly. "Didn't I mention that she was coming over? She loves my lemon meringue pie."

She's probably still trying to buy my bike, Rain thought.

Three days later, Rain sent his applications to the business schools. One month later, he was accepted by his top choice. Two years later, the paperboy earned his second M.B.A.

THE RAIN READER

—

Thank you for reading, *Rain: What a Paperboy Learned About Business*. As you have learned, Rain is a plucky, confident teenager who is destined for business and personal success. Each of Rain's adventures and each of the book's chapters are full of messages, learnings, and business and life lessons. "The Rain Reader" is designed to stimulate analysis, thinking, and discussion on problem solving, entrepreneurship, making money, leadership, taking personal responsibility, creativity, marketing, innovation, respect for mentors and parents, and much more. *Rain* is both simple and complex.

Following is a series of analytical exercises anchored in each of Rain's adventures. The exercises are designed to illuminate Rain's entrepreneurial thinking and his rainmaking principles. See how you might retool these principles for your organization and your personal career growth.

Get Up

Successful people, working men and women, be they bricklayers or brick makers, hedge trimmers or hedge fund managers, car washers or car manufacturers, working moms or stay-at-home moms, have one thing in common: they work. Successful people go to the store, to the factory, to the job. They venture on to the playing field. They go into the courtroom, the classroom, the hospital room, the locker room, the dining room, the baby's room, the boardroom. They go into the fray uncertain but confident, fearful but fearless, overwhelmed but willing. Successful people suck it up and do what has to be done. They take their shots. They take their bruises and breaks. They get up. They show up. They win more than they lose. Getting up is the first step to success.

Exercise

Everyone knows you have to get up to show up. Often, showing up late is equivalent to not showing up at all. Everyone knows that being chronically late is bad business and bad manners. Yet some people are late, or too late, too often. Managers who have been successful in changing the tardy have done so using specific examples, and then quantifying and dollarizing the negative impact of the examples. The worksheet uses common late events to demonstrate the quantification and dollar-ization technique. Add in other examples from your experience.

How can you use this technique, or adaptations to improve productivity, in your organization?

_____

_____

_____

_____

_____

_____

_____

_____

_____

_____

_____

_____

_____

_____

_____

_____

_____

_____

_____

Event	Quantification	Dollarization	Management Options
Late for scheduled meetings	Late for a total of twenty minutes for three monthlies involving five others in each meeting	Six people (five waiting plus latecomer) times 20 minutes times $1.00 per minute (average per minute compensation of attendees times three meetings). $6 \times 20 \times \$1 = \$360$	"Should we deduct $360 from your paycheck?"
Late for airplane flight	One missed flight. One minimum parking charge. Three hours travel time wasted. One deal lost.	Missed flight penalty, $100 Parking charge, $15 180 minutes × $1.00, $180 Lost deal, $10,000	"If someone else cost your company $10,295 what would you do?"
Late for class	Five minutes late for company-paid graduate course. Misses professor's outline of final exam. Scores 72 versus class average of 88. Final grade 85, or B.	Company pays 100 percent times $1,000 course price for a grade of A. Pays 80 percent for B. Tardy employees must pay $200.	"Not showing up on time cost you $40 a minute. How many more minutes can you afford to lose?"

Opportunity

An opportunity is the chance to make something good happen. Opportunities abound, but they are not always obvious, and an opportunity perfect for one person or for an organization may be irrelevant to others. An opportunity is just a chance, not an outcome. Opportunists are action people who capitalize on the chance. Successful opportunists are those who recognize the chance, develop a plan, and find the fortitude to execute. Successful people don't dither, don't dally, don't delay. Successful people *do*.

Exercise

1. What does your company do to recognize and quantify opportunity?

   _____

   _____

2. What is your company's attitude toward doing what it takes to capitalize on opportunity?

   _____

   _____

   _____

3. How has your company prospered or suffered from taking advantage of opportunity or from passing?

Use one or two specific examples to frame your
analysis.

Took Advantage and Dollar Value	Passed and Dollars Missed
_____	_____
_____	_____

4. What should your company do to increase its
   opportunities? Your list may include investment in
   R&D, customer research, more salespeople, and
   so forth.

   Recommendations to Increase Opportunity

   _____

   _____

   _____

   _____

Interview Planning

A job interview is a sales call. The interviewee is the salesperson and the product. People interview for jobs at organizations to pursue a full-time career. People who sell professional services, such as consultants and lawyers, interview potential clients to get hired to do a project. Because a job interview is a sales call, it must be preplanned. The job candidate must do research to determine what the hiring person, the customer, wants. The job candidate, the salesperson, must preplan the questions to ask, the possible customer objections to overcome, ways to wow the customer.

One thing rainmakers do that ordinary salespeople rarely do is to preplan every sales call and to do so in writing. Rainmakers know that precall research often uncovers a clue, a fact—something that, if deftly presented, can close the deal. Rainmakers believe that 90 percent of all sales calls are won or lost in precall planning.

Exercise

1. Does every one of the salespeople in your organization precall-plan every sales call on decision makers? If not, what might your company do to institute this crucial selling discipline?

   _____

   _____

2. Given your customers, your sales cycle, and how
   your customers decide to buy, what items must be
   included in a precall planner? Best-practice planners include sales call objective, decision makers'
   names, customer budget, and timetable. What
   fifteen or twenty other considerations should be
   included in your company's precall planners?

   _____

   _____

   _____

   _____

Interview

A job interview is a sales call. Characteristics of a quality sales call include calling on the decision maker, having a precall plan, anticipating customer questions and concerns, and, of course, asking for the order, that is, asking for the job.

Asking for the order is one thing that rainmakers do that ordinary salespeople rarely, if ever, do. Rainmakers know that asking for the order provides a competitive advantage. This is because up to 95 percent of all salespeople, depending on the industry, never ask for the order.

Great salespeople listen more than they talk. Rainmakers ask prepared, practiced questions. They love to show something on a sales call that demonstrates their homework, their knowledge about something particularly interesting or challenging to the customer.

Rain asked Mr. D'Michaels for the job three times. If 90 to 95 percent of all salespeople rarely or never ask for the order, what percentage of all salespeople ask more than once on a call? What percentage will ask if they hear no or the customer equivocates? The answer is: "only salespeople who preplan and are prepared to hear no!"

Exercise

1. Why do you think so few salespeople ask for customer commitments, ask for the sale?

_____

2. What can your organization do to get the salespeople to ask for customer commitments?

_____

_____

3. Rain showed Mr. D'Michaels the results of his market research, and he showed a practical solution to a problem: the coin changer. What do your salespeople show the customer? What could, or should, they show the customer?

_____

_____

4. Do an anatomy of one of the best sales calls in your organization. What did the salesperson do, and how can those actions be taught to others?

   Elements of the Best Sales Call

_____

_____

_____

_____

Money

Killjoys are always quoting, "Money is the root of all evil." The killjoys have the quote wrong. The correct line is, "The love of money is the root of all evil." Isn't "the root of all evil" a little strong? Is money the root of deadly viruses, drought, mental illness, child abuse? And if someone hadn't made a bit of money and donated it to science, we would still have polio.

The most acceptable pursuits (of money) are hard work and risking and investing time and capital. Inheriting money, winning the lottery, and successfully suing somebody are not as worthy as reaping the fruits of one's labor.

Exercise

1. Rain has a focus on making money to buy things and to save. Corporations have a focus on making money to reward investors and repay lenders, to pay employees and suppliers. Nonprofit organizations have a focus on raising money to fund their mission, to stay alive. What do you think your employees think about the notion of making money? What do the leaders, the owners, or shareholders, think?

Employees' Views	Shareholders' Views
_____	_____
_____	_____

2. If you need to reconcile these views to achieve common business goals, what *should* you do? List three initiatives.

(a) _____

(b) _____

(c) _____

The Dinner Table

For as long as there have been families, the dinner table is where parents and extended families have taught their children through example. The dinner table is the first classroom. It is where kids learn manners, to ask and answer questions, to interact with adults, to participate, to help. The dinner table is where moms and dads engage their children, elicit opinions, teach the art of conversation, tell old stories. It is also where people get to meet and know strangers, new friends, customers, potential partners. The dinner table is where deals are done, decisions are made.

Exercise

1. What life-lasting lessons did you learn at your favorite dinner table?

   _____

   _____

2. What lessons do you think every kid should learn at the dinner table?

   _____

3. Can leadership be taught, or learned, at the dinner table?

   _____

Day One

Day One is about finishing what you start. Lots of jobs are tough, especially in the first few days and weeks. Jobs can be physically tough, emotionally stressful, and have a hostile work environment. But tough is not an acceptable reason for anyone to quit. And tough competitors, tough markets, or tough times are not reasons for a company to hunker down, to pull back, to quit the marketplace. Unless the company has a 100 percent market share, for every product, there is still business available regardless of downturns.

Day One is about taking responsibility for getting the job done and for doing what you signed up to do.

Exercise

1. What tough time, if any, have you endured, and what did you do to persevere?

   _____

2. What tough environments does your company face? What ideas do you have to overcome the tough circumstances?

Challenges	Action Ideas

3. How will you lead your company to implement your ideas?

   _____

Mean Dogs

As all plaintiff lawyers know, mean dogs are real. In *Rain*, the mean dogs are a metaphor for other perils— attackers, scary things in the night, things that are unreasonable or illogical, purveyors of terror. Mean dogs are manifest in life and in business. They can be enemy combatants, ruthless competitors, plotting colleagues (as Julius Caesar foretold when he said, "Yon Cassius has a lean and hungry look"), hurtful gossips, and random predators.

In *Rain*, the vicious beast was a huge, unmistakable presence. In life, the vicious beast is not always visible. In life and in business, the meanest of dogs may be cunning, patient, amoral, pathological, skillful, able. That mean dogs exist is the raison d'être for police, intelligence agencies, business planners, and courageous leaders.

Exercise

1. Who or what are the mean dogs in your business? They may be irrational customers, ill-intentioned coworkers, a bad boss, unscrupulous competitors, overzealous regulators. List the mean dogs, if any in the first column after the next question.

2. Next to each mean dog, write down what you believe is their motivation. What do they really want? Better customer service? Your job? More

money? More recognition? Power? For each, think
of a constructive solution. What is the doggie treat
that will make them love you (and 90 percent
will)? For the other 10 percent—that mean dog,
visible or invisible, leaping at the fence—what
hamburger, that is, what mental jujitsu, can you
employ to neutralize this mean dog?

Mean Dog Challenge	Mean Dog's Motivation	Solution Ideas
_____	_____	_____
_____	_____	_____
_____	_____	_____
_____	_____	_____
_____	_____	_____

The Ten Customer Commandments

Customers, customers, customers. Without customers, there are no sales, no revenues, no tips, no baseball cards, no movies, no bikes. They expect to get what they paid for and are delighted when they get a little bit more. Customers care only about their needs, and care not a whit about the seller's needs. Customers want what they want when they want it.

Customers are so important to every person in every organization that stamping paychecks with a note, "This Is Customer Money," is a startling reminder that without customers or patients, or parishioners, or members, the organization dies. All employees must know with perfect clarity how they directly or indirectly get and keep customers.

Exercise

1. What customer commandments have you, or your company, posted?

2. What other customer commandments are appropriate for Rain or for your company? List twenty new commandments.

The Twenty Commandments

_____

_____

_____

_____

_____

_____

_____

_____

_____

_____

_____

_____

_____

_____

_____

_____

_____

_____

_____

_____

The Sundays

One reason that being a paperboy or papergirl is so demanding and so formative is that it requires mental, physical, and emotional strength. It is hard work, and relatively harder for a kid than an adult. "The Sundays" is about tough times—when circumstances are overwhelming and one's capacities appear insufficient. Tough times make tough people. Hard times make hard people. Tough times are often crucibles of leadership (revisit the names in this book's preface). Facing the challenge, persevering, taking best shots, and not leaving the fray make good times.

In this chapter, Rain also learned about the decency and fairness that characterize the vast majority of customers. In dealing with your customer base, remember that most play fairly and act decently. Rain also learned the importance of personal handwritten notes.

Exercise

1. What "Sundays," what fixable problems, are hindering your organization?

   _____

   _____

2. What solutions can you offer your organization?

   _____

   _____

3. What tasks or initiatives in your organization strike you as high effort and low impact?

_____

_____

_____

4. What should you do as a leader, as Rain did, to find a better way?

_____

_____

_____

5. What problems do you see other companies' employees struggling with every day? Do you see salespeople patiently explaining to customers about chronic and late deliveries? Do you see soldiers with insufficient equipment? Do you see the busy bartender who runs out of ice? Do you see the frantic and the frenzied without the proper tools, with inadequate training, lacking enough people to get the job done?

_____

_____

_____

_____

6. What can we learn from Rain about problem solving, taking responsibility, turning mud into money?

_____

_____

_____

7. In this e-age, how might a handwritten note distinguish you and your company?

_____

_____

_____

_____

Referrals

Using referrals to get new business, new customers, and new sales might be the most effective of all selling strategies. The arithmetic of the referral dynamics tells the story. A salesperson who asks ten influential referral sources for a referral will, on average, get seven referrals. Of the seven referrals, about 60 percent will qualify as real prospects. If the subsequent selling process is executed properly, 75 percent of the prospects will buy. And if the new customers buy, say, $500 of product a year for three and a half years, then each customer is worth $1,750. Thus, asking one hundred referral sources yields seventy referrals, which yields forty-two qualified prospects, which yields thirty to thirty-two sales. At $1,750 in revenue per customer, the referral-asking salesperson generates $52,500 in total revenues. And as the infomercials shout, "There's more!" The thirty new customers will generate twenty-one referrals, and so on, and so on.

Rain's Referral Money Math

1. Start with the number of referral resources.

   _____

2. Multiply the number of referral sources (say, 100, for this example) by 70 percent, which is, on average, the number of referrals that will come from

the referral sources. (You will get the names of seventy potential customers).

---

3. Multiply the number of potential customers (in this case, 70 potentials) times 60 percent, which is, on average, the number of referrals that will be qualified prospects (60 percent × 70 = 42 qualified prospects).

---

4. Multiply the number of qualified prospects (42) times 75 percent, which is, on average, the number of prospects who become actual customers (75 percent × 42 = 30 to 32 new customers).

---

5. Multiply the number of new customers times the average revenue value of the customer in one year. This gives you the first-year value of the new customer.

---

6. Multiply the average number of years you keep the customer times the average annual revenue value of the customer. This gives you the total annuity revenue value of each new customer.

---

7. Multiply the average annuity value of one customer times the number of new customers, and this gives you the revenue value of the original pool of referral sources.

Given the power of referrals, it is stunning that no more than 10 percent of all salespeople actually execute the entire process from asking for a referral to asking the customer to buy. The primary reason that ordinary salespeople don't ask is that they fear rejection. Rainmakers fear rejection as well, but they take a deep breath and ask anyway. The irony is that rainmakers are rejected a hundred times more than ordinary salespeople because rainmakers ask and others don't.

Exercise

1. It is reckoned that at least 90 percent of all salespeople never ask the customer for the business, never ask for any customer commitment that would lead to an order, and never even ask for a referral. What can your organization do to motivate and enable your salespeople to ask for customer commitments and increase close rates?

_____

_____

_____

_____

2. Make a list of ten clients you feel would be likely
   to give referrals.

   _____   _____

   _____   _____

   _____   _____

   _____   _____

   _____   _____

3. What's in it for referral sources to provide you
   with referrals?

   _____

   _____

   _____

4. Rain asked _The Gazette_ to "spring for one week of
   free papers." What is the annuity revenue value of
   a new customer to _The Gazette?_ What is the annuity value of a new customer to your organization?

   _____

   _____

   _____

5. Use Rain's Referral Money Math formula for your
   ten referral sources (question 2 above). Given
   your company's average dollar sale and average
   annuity life of the customer relationship, what
   does "Money Math" predict for you?

   _____

   _____

   _____

   _____

   _____

   _____

   _____

   _____

   _____

The Contest

There are four elements used to develop compensation plans for salespeople: base salary, commissions, bonuses, and the monetary value of prizes won. All compensation plans are a combination of one or all of these factors. The highest-paid salespeople, the rainmakers, are paid on performance, defined as profitable revenues generated. Rainmakers may work for companies where they are paid entirely or primarily on commission, such as stockbrokers, insurance agents, real estate agents, and paperboys. Rainmakers may work for themselves or in a company that appreciates and appropriately pays them for the profitable revenues they generate. These rainmakers are often business owners, law firm partners, sports agents, manufacturing representatives. Essentially rainmakers are paid on commissions. They are like the solitary farmer, fisherman, and hunter: they eat only what they grow, catch, or kill.

Most rainmakers, the highest-earning salespeople, don't see themselves competing with other salespeople. Most toil alone in small businesses. They would rather make money than win contests. (But rainmakers do win contests, and they gladly snatch the prize.)

That rainmakers don't see themselves as competing against other companies does not mean that they are not competitive. Rainmakers hate to lose. Rain-makers are winners.

Exercise

1. Are contests effective in motivating salespeople? Why? Why not?

_____

_____

_____

2. Are contests more effective with, say, rainmakers, or superperformers, than with less successful sales-people? Why do you think so?

_____

_____

_____

3. What incentives does your company use, if any? Are they effective?

_____

_____

_____

4. The best incentives are those directly linked to improving performance. How would you charac-terize your incentive use?

_____

_____

5. What incentives should your company use, or test, or reprise?

_____

_____

6. Rain's selling at Pops's Diner is a "get" strategy. He got new Gazette customers. (The Coffee Corner promotion was a customer "keep" strategy.) What effective get strategies does your organization employ? What get strategies should you try?

_____

_____

_____

7. Rain seals the deal with Pops with a handshake. This is an iconic American deal notion, but is it smart? What do you think of handshake deals versus written contracts? What do handshake deals say about the handshakers?

_____

_____

_____

Luck

"Luck," of course, is not about being lucky. It is not a reflection of the aphorism, "The harder I work, the luckier I get." (Rain would process that conceit and undoubtedly think, "How lucky are those hard-working galley slaves when the ship's captain wants to go waterskiing?") "Luck" is about accomplishment and the rewards that accompany accomplishment. "Luck" is about being fortunate, and modest enough to accept one's fortune.

Exercise

1. You may feel blessed for all the good things that have come your way. For this exercise, list your blessings that you can chalk up to true luck, and list those produced by planning, or sacrifice, or work, or risk taking, or prudence. The latter list will be the longest.

Planning	Sacrifice	Risk Taking	Prudence
_____	_____	_____	_____
_____	_____	_____	_____
_____	_____	_____	_____
_____	_____	_____	_____
_____	_____	_____	_____

2. What new activities can you adopt, new projects to undertake, that might increase your luck? That might increase your company's luck?

_____

_____

_____

Bonus

The best bonus is the surprise bonus—one not tied to rules and policies and not tied to a time of the year. Surprise bonuses energize. They are also a window into a company's culture and management. Bonuses indicate that the company is making money and is willing to reinvest into its employees. Surprise bonuses mean that management is not overly constrained by work rules and human resource department dictates. The surprise bonus shows that leadership can deal with ambiguity, that everything need not be spelled out. The surprise bonus is always proof that in good organizations, a person who does good things will get noticed.

Exercise

1. Surprise bonuses are untidy, but they are highly motivating to the recipient. If you agree with surprise bonuses, what kinds of policies might your organization employ to make them available?

Pros	Cons

2. How might your company create more effective bonuses to promote desired outcomes?

The Bully (Part I)

The Chuckie Moriartys of the world, and their female equivalents, are a common little kid's fear: the bigger, stronger, hurtful bully. Though the world's literature generally relegates the bully to the playground, adults also fear the bully. Bullies are real, and they exist in schools, in the military, in the neighborhood, among tribes, at work, in families.

Bullies are bullies only because they have greater physical power or economic power or the power of higher rank. Without such power, bullies won't bully. But the certain reality is that bullies immorally take advantage of their greater power.

Although the bullied hate the bully, many accept the bully. Though the unbullied hate the bully, many will let it go. Some of the bullied will fight back, and most will lose the fight (a lesson the bully knows well). For those bullied in an organization, be aware that you are probably not alone. That you are being bullied does not go unnoticed. Keep records. Every time there is an incident, write down dates, facts, names, numbers. A truthful, proof-filled, fact-filled written record is the best weapon if you choose to confront. There will be supporters. The bully will buckle.

161

Exercise

1. Do you know of a circumstance where a bully or a bullying activity was neutralized or eliminated? What actions were taken to stop the bullying?

2. If there is a bully in your life, you can choose to neutralize the bully, protect yourself, or escape. A bully's actions can be subtle and hard for others to detect. Bullying actions can happen in private, avoiding witnesses. Start a file, a journal, to record and capture every incident, every word. Keep contemporaneous notes. Document everything. Write down the incident, the date, time, place, people. Capture seemingly trivial details. A factual record is your best weapon against a bully and will influence those with greater power than the bully. If there is a bully in your life, start your journal today.

Green Lightning

"Green Lightning" is about far more than a kid's bicycle. Green Lightning is about doing the ordinary with flair. Green Lightning is about clever flamboyance, leaving an unforgettable impression. Green Lightning is Mayor Fiorello ("Little Flower") La Guardia's omnipresent boutonnieres, P. T. Barnum's painted circus train, the Texas Cadillac car dealer's longhorned-festooned El Dorado, Lee Flaherty's Flair House in Chicago.

Green Lightning is also about marketing and innovation, the only two sustaining factors in every business.

Ernest and Julio Gallo created the market for popular wines in the United States. Ernest was the marketing genius and Julio the wine-making genius. They started E&J Gallo by themselves, and they were the only two employees. Their business model was simple: Ernest would sell all the wines Julio made, and Julio would make all the wines Ernest sold.

Exercise

1. Rain and Ellis were partners in the creation of Green Lightning. How would you characterize their different roles?

   _____

   _____

_____

_____

2. Rain knew he lacked mechanical know-how.
   What can managers learn from Rain's partnering
   with Ellis? How does the Rain-Ellis partnership
   inform your thinking on delegation, teamwork,
   trusting others' expertise, and giving up control?

   _____

   _____

   _____

3. What can your organization do to stand out in a
   crowded marketplace?

   _____

   _____

   _____

Innovation

Customer problems are one of the petri dishes of innovation. (Business problems, competitor actions, and marketplace changes are also petri dishes.) Any new thing that improves a customer situation is new, or innovative, to that customer. Innovation can take place in any part of a company's business, from product development to delivering the product to answering the phone.

Innovators are listeners, observers. They question, tinker, dare, risk, plan, test, try. They recognize when customers have learned to live with a suboptimal product. They know that it is difficult for customers to rate or evaluate situation-changing innovations. (It is reported that when Steven Ballmer, now Microsoft CEO, told his mother he was going into the computer industry, Mrs. Ballmer asked, "Why would anyone need a computer?")

The pace of innovation increases when leadership prods and rewards innovation; when the marketers are in the marketplace instead of in meetings; when companies hire creative people; when CEO's kill the idea killers.

The innovator sees more than the problem; he or she also sees the challenge, sees the opportunity, sees the solution. Lots of people and companies know the answer. The innovator gets it done and makes the solution a reality.

Exercise

1. After the customer explained what he wanted, Rain's answer was an immediate, "Yes, I can." Was that smart or not? Why?

   _____

2. If Rain were working for a big corporation and a customer asked for something extra that would cost extra, how would Rain's "Yes, I can," be considered?

   _____

3. The Gazette sold each paper to Rain for fifteen cents. Assume that its cost of producing each paper was, say, ten cents. Thus, if the plastic wrap cost only a cent, it would increase *The Gazette*'s product costs by 10 percent. A 10 percent increase in costs without an increase in selling price is huge. What do you think might be the pro and con arguments inside your organization if you were to do for all your customers something akin to what Rain was doing for his customers?

Pros	Cons
_____	_____
_____	_____
_____	_____

4. How many weather-damaged papers, and their attendant cost of replacement, would it take for *The Gazette* to break even on its investment in improved product quality?

_____

5. How does investing in innovation, in quality, in customer service raise profits?

_____

6. Can you think of examples in your organization where money invested in improved quality gave a positive return on investment (ROI)?

_____

7. Can you identify areas in your organization where investing money to improve quality would have a long-term positive ROI? Can you calculate that ROI?

_____

8. Is it smart to say yes to take the business, without any idea if you are going to fulfill the promise? Why yes? Why not?

_____

9. What might be the outcome if Rain had politely said, "I don't think so?"

_____

_____

Coffee

"Coffee" is about being on high-receive, always aware, always customer-centric. Many people, even smart and intelligent people, are blind to the obvious. Some are blinded by adherence to convention, tradition, prejudice, preconceptions. Myopic people miss the obvious because they accept the cliché. They don't question. They believe in myths. Some people tied to a previous decision or to a routine or pattern will fight the obvious, fight the facts. It is much more fun to suspend disbelief when watching a magician. To see the obvious, it is best to suspend belief.

Rain sees that coffee, muffins, doughnuts, and the morning newspaper are interrelated, or could be. To Rain, the linkage is obvious, and it is a marketing opportunity.

The long definition of *marketing* is the profitable identification, attraction, getting, and keeping of okay customers. Rain's Coffee Corner promotion is primarily designed to keep his customers. Rain figures that by sponsoring the free muffin, he will engender more customer loyalty, making it easier to keep the customer, and perhaps promoting goodwill word-of-mouth advertising to get more customers.

Exercise

1. What customer-keeping activities does your organization do?

   _____

   _____

2. What kinds of keep activities should you introduce?

   _____

   _____

3. Marketers call the Coffee Corner/*Gazette* coupon idea a cobranded promotion. Why are cobranded promotions usually very effective?

   _____

   _____

4. The Coffee Corner coupon promotion cost very little money. What might be the economic returns to the Coffee Corner, to *The Gazette*, and to Rain?

   _____

   _____

5. Are there any low-cost simple marketing ideas your company should do to get and keep okay customers?

   _____

   _____

Rookie

"Rookie" is about winners, not winning. Winners such as Rain are so because they are always thinking of others. Winners are thankful and understand that they didn't win without help. Winners are generous with praise, with credit, and to giving others what's due them. Winners always leave something on the table for the other guy. Winners know that "when it's all about them, I win. When it's all about me, I lose."

Exercise

1. Winning Rookie of the Year is often an accurate predictor of future career success. Take Major League Baseball: Rod Carew was Rookie of the Year, and he's in the Hall of Fame. Other rookies who are now Hall of Famers include Eddie Murray, Cal Ripken Jr., Jackie Robinson, and Willie Mays. Pete Rose should be in the Hall. Derek Jeter will be. And the same is true in football, basketball, car racing, and horse racing. Rookies of the Year are winners. What does a rookie in your organization have to do to win Rookie of the Year, whether you bestow that award or not?

   _____

   _____

2. Consider the high performers in your organizations—rookies and seasoned veterans. What do the high performers do that others should be doing?

_____

_____

3. Corporations rarely bestow Rookie of the Year awards. Why do you think that is the case? Are organizations unable to accurately measure everyone's performance? Are there other challenges? Should there be more corporate Rookies of the Year?

   Yes, and Why   **No, and Why Not**

   _____   _____

   _____   _____

4. Rain gives his gift certificate to his mother. How is that gesture typical of great salespeople, of those who know that selling inside is often the most important sale?

_____

_____

Photo

Other than word-of-mouth advertising and other than
the one-in-a-million breakthrough commercial or ad,
backed by huge spending budgets, the best way to build
positive brand awareness is through publicity. Good
publicity is hard to get. (Bad publicity is much easier to
get.) The formula for great publicity has these factors:
memorable story, emotional hook, audience relevance,
and media-friendly images. Publicity builds brands in
different ways than do advertising, promotion, and direct
selling. As opposed to, say, a commercial or sales pitch,
readers, listeners, and viewers *voluntarily* consume publicity. The pictures of entertainers on magazines cause
people to buy, then read. The customer who voluntarily invests money and time in publicity stories tends to
believe those stories, is influenced by the stories, and
has greater recall of the message than if experienced
through advertising. An ad of Rain wearing his baseball
uniform would generate far less interest, readership, and
paper sales than the "cute kid makes good" story.

Exercise

1. It is a huge oversimplification, but it can be argued
   that there are two end points on the spectrum
   called "marketing person" or "innovator." At one
   end is the completely intuitive marketer, and at

the other is the totally data-driven marketer. What might be a workable definition of both types of marketers? What characteristics best describe each?

_____

_____

_____

2. What type of marketer is the most effective in your organization? Why?

_____

_____

_____

3. What type of marketer is the best at discovering and filling customers' unarticulated needs? Why?

_____

_____

_____

4. Why does Rain insist on wearing his baseball uniform? Would other kids have done the same, or would they dress conventionally?

_____

_____

_____

5. Can you think of potentially sensational marketing ideas or new products or crazy publicity events that were aborted because they weren't conventional? What about next time?

_____

_____

_____

_____

Crime and Punishment

Though skipping school doesn't rank with theft, it is a rule, a law, that makes societal sense. Rain was wrong in breaking this rule. However, does it make sense for managers, entrepreneurs, and companies to obey all the rules, the policies, the rock-hard myths, the theories that abound in business? Industry needs rule breakers, challengers of conventional thinking. Companies need innovators. Fred Smith's 1963 Yale University term paper that outlined a new business model for overnight delivery of packages, and which became the blueprint for Federal Express, got a grade of below average.

Some rules are there for our protection, and some fetter creativity and productivity. The trick is knowing which rules can be broken. Generally, if what the entrepreneur or innovator wants to do is not against the laws of God or state, then try it.

Challenging the way things are done can be good if it's done constructively. If you are brave enough to be a rule breaker, you have to be prepared to accept the consequences of your actions and, of course, to accept the rewards.

Exercise

1. Should organizations, particularly big ones, tolerate benevolent rule breakers? Why, or why not?

_____

_____

2. How should organizations balance the need for breakthrough thinkers (aka rule breakers) with the concomitant need for order and process?

_____

_____

3. What policies and rules in your workplace fetter creativity or discourage individuality?

_____

_____

4. What policies or rules in your organization, if broken, cause no harm?

_____

_____

5. As a leader, what must you do to stimulate innovation?

_____

_____

Collections

Every job in every company, without exception, must be directly or indirectly tied to getting and keeping customers. This includes the job of collecting late payments from customers. Too many organizations treat their late-paying customers as deadbeats. (Even deadbeat customers must be treated with courtesy and respect.) Too many organizations dun their late-paying customers, assign customers to voracious debt collectors, even cut off service. Some of the large oil companies temporarily freeze or cancel their customer's charge card if the customer is late in paying. Does the "card-denied" customer drop to her knees and wail by the gas pump, or does she use another credit card or go to another gas station? One thing is for sure: she is going to buy gas, and the oil company loses the sale, and potentially the customer.

If you had a plumber fix your toilet and you forgot to pay the bill, or you are late over ninety days, and your pipe springs a leak, who are you going to call? You are going to call a new plumber. If the first plumber found a way for the customer to pay some amount, put the customer on a payment plan, for example, and was unflaggingly polite and courteous, chances are better that the customer would hire the plumber to fix the broken pipe. The plumber of course has the option to

177

decline the business or to get a stronger guarantee or payment before fixing the pipe.

Collecting from good customers keeps good customers.

Exercise

1. Why didn't Rain simply stop delivering the paper to the politics house?

_____

2. If Rain hadn't delivered the paper, what would the customer do?

_____

3. How much money is the customer worth to Rain?

_____

4. How is Rain's collections problem solution like his "mean dogs" solution?

_____

5. Rain (and Vern) fashion a plan that had the man walk down the driveway. Comment below on the pros and cons of their strategy.

For example, possible pros

1. It is an advantage to negotiate on one's turf (the driveway).

_____

2. The customer might come to understand that delivering papers in nasty weather is tough work.

3. Rain's seller's leverage, withholding the paper, is strengthened by being distant from the house, accompanied by Vern.

For example, possible cons

1. By discomfiting the customer, making him walk in the rain, doesn't Rain break a good customer service rule?

2. If the customer feels Rain took unfair advantage, what might he do to punish Rain?

3. Adult behavior might call for having a civilized conversation on the customer's porch. Is doing otherwise poor business practice?

Ice

"Ice" is also about "unintended consequences," the cliché favored by inept, incompetent, and small thinkers. "Unintended consequences" is an excuse used to airily wave away the negative aftermaths of bad planning and bad decision making. Because "unintended consequences" sounds so erudite, its blithe use is to both shield and shroud the culprit. But unintended consequences are really the result of not thinking things through, not considering all outcomes, and not asking, "What if?"

"Ice" is also about taking shortcuts. Good shortcuts can cut costs, time, and risk. Bad shortcuts can cost and cost and cost.

Frostbite, pneumonia, hypothermia, possible death are probable consequences, be they intended or unintended, of falling into any body of frigid water in freezing winter weather.

"Ice" is about staying calm in a crisis.

Exercise

1. If Rain had not fallen, would his decision to take the shortcut be okay?

_____

_____

2. What if Rain had successfully taken the same shortcut ten times earlier? Would his decision still be okay or not okay?

_____

3. About crossing freezing water on an icy log, should we cut the teenager Rain any slack?

_____

4. If crossing the brook does save time, what might Rain do?

_____

5. Can you identify shortcuts taken in your organization and evaluate the outcomes?

_____

_____

_____

6. Is there a way for the people in your organization to identify shortcuts and objectively evaluate the payoffs and consequences of taking or not taking the shortcut?

_____

_____

_____

Exit Strategy and Valuation

Every ongoing business is ultimately sold. It may be sold within the family, to private interests, to another company, or to open market shareholders. But every business is sold. The dynamics of selling a business—timing, pricing, buyer selection, negotiation, and much more—are all factors for the owner who is planning an exit strategy to consider.

Crucially important to a successful business sale is for the seller to have a good idea of what the enterprise is worth. The seller can price the business at any level, but to execute a successful negotiation, the seller must understand the value.

Exercise

1. What factors are crucial to determining the value of your company, your new product, your career?

_____

_____

2. Knowing how a company makes money is the first step in valuing a company. How does your company make money?

_____

_____

3. Which products are your most profitable? Why?

_____

_____

_____

4. Which customers are making you money or losing you money? Why?

_____

_____

_____

5. At what revenues does your company break even?

_____

_____

6. What do you think your company is worth?

_____

_____

Negotiation

Marketing is the identification, attraction, getting, and keeping of customers. One important part of the marketing mix is selling. Negotiation is one type of selling. A negotiation has a buyer and a seller. The seller might be someone selling a house or a paper route. The buyer is the potential purchaser of the house or the paper route.

A negotiation is often the last phase in the selling process. The negotiation begins after the seller has agreed to sell, the buyer has agreed to buy, and both parties know it. Negotiations can fail, but generally reaching the negotiation phase means that a deal, imperfect, or not, is going to happen.

Good negotiators, be they sellers or buyers, never accept the first offer, regardless of its attractiveness. To accept the first offer signals to the other side that they might have done better. This leads to seller's or buyer's remorse, which can cause a deal to unravel.

Exercise

1. There is always customer pressure on the seller's price. How would you rate your organization's ability to negotiate selling prices?

   _____

   _____

2. How would you rate your company's performance on negotiating contracts, partnerships, hirings, terminations?

_____

_____

3. Notice how the new kid compliments Rain. Why is that technique important in negotiations?

_____

_____

4. Rain sealed the "Contest" deal with Pops with a handshake. He seals selling his route with a handshake, and with the "deal maker's contract," the napkin. Why does Rain want a written contract?

_____

_____

5. List five tactics you intend to employ to effect a good outcome in an upcoming negotiation.

_____

_____

_____

The New Kid

Selling the paper route, like selling any other business, is one exit strategy for small business owners. The seller needs to be sure that the buyer has the money. The seller needs to be sure that if all the purchase price is not paid at closing, the buyer will pay any balance at agreed-to times in the future. Responsible sellers want to ensure that all stakeholders are well served after the sale. In Rain's case, the important stakeholders are *The Gazette*, the customers, the buyer, the buyer's parents, and his parents. Thus, the choice of buyer is not a casual decision.

There are other pressures on a seller. All owed money, if any, must be repaid. All records must be accurate and passed to the buyer. The new kid has to be trained to give the customers what they have come to expect. Customer expectations have to be managed. Customers should not be surprised. There must be an event-free passing of *The Gazette* newspaper carry bag. Other interested buyers who were not selected should be appeased, as some are undoubtedly friends of Rain.

Exercise

1. One factor, usually important to getting promoted in an organization, is to have a ready, able, and recognized successor. What can you learn about

getting promoted or succession planning from the selling company exit strategy?

_____

_____

2. One of Rain's constraints in selling his business was the need for continuity of the business, so as to not interrupt delivery service. How is that constraint similar to an organization's succession planning?

_____

_____

3. What would be important to potential buyers or your organization?

_____

_____

4. What interview questions should the seller ask any interested buyer?

_____

_____

_____

The Bully (Part II)

Bullies bully because they can, because they have superior power, and because they are not nice people. Bullies fear the loss of their power. They fear exposure, witnesses, and having to deal with a superior power. Bullies in the workplace can be a dominating competitor, a monopolistic supplier, a hurtful boss, a huge and arrogant customer. Standing up to a bully is always an act of courage. In business, managers have to judge the economic consequences of standing up to, for example, that large customer using its buying power to drive down prices and profits. They have to judge the impact of changing suppliers. Leaders have to devise clever strategies to gain market share from dominating competitors. Leaders can't allow long-term bullying, or their organization will be imperiled.

Exercise

1. Identify any bullies in your sphere.

   _____

   _____

2. What is the source of each bully's power?

   _____

   _____

3. What might the bully fear? What are possible
   bully weaknesses?

   _____

   _____

4. What is the quality of your market intelligence?

   _____

5. What evidence, marketplace activities, or data
   might indicate or signal a change in the bully's
   power position?

   _____

   _____

   _____

Vern

Vern is the rock. He is always there. Vern is knowing. He is not a confabulator. He is *costaud*. (Look them up—the latter in a French-English dictionary.) Vern is the ultimate go-to guy. He is the person all smart and ambitious kids wish they knew, or feel blessed that they do know. Given all the teachers, coaches, mentors, and role models in your life, how many were outstanding, memorably influential? Everybody should have a Vern in the shadows and in the trenches. As the saying goes, "Vern had Rain's back."

Exercise

1. What can you learn from Vern and use in leading people who report to you?

   _____

   _____

2. What can other leaders or mentors in your organization learn from Vern?

   _____

   _____

3. If you were Vern's manager how would you "manage" him, treat him, use him?

   _____

   _____

Getting an M.B.A.

Being a paperboy is no different than owning or running a business. The successful paperboy is an entrepreneur, a marketer, a leader, a salesperson, a distributor, a bill collector, and more. Every job, every work experience, at any career stage is full of lessons. In every job, you learn about good and bad bosses, working with colleagues, getting things done with others, using outside expertise. Every day offers the ambitious and the smart a chance to learn something new.

Exercise

1. What one, two, or three lessons in Rain are important to you?

   _____

   _____

2. How will you use those lessons to further your success?

   _____

   _____

3. Countless paperboys and papergirls attribute their career success to the lessons they learned delivering papers. What early job experiences, good or bad, have influenced your career?

   _____

   _____

4. What are you going to do today, tonight, or tomorrow to supercharge your life, your leadership, your career?

_____

_____

EPILOGUE

Thank you for investing your time and intellect into this story. May you benefit a thousand times.

Jeffrey J. Fox

ABOUT THE AUTHOR

Jeffrey J. Fox is an accomplished consultant, popular speaker, and the acclaimed author of a series of hard-hitting international business best-sellers, including *How to Become a Rainmaker* and *How to Become CEO*. Prior to founding Fox & Company, Inc., a premier marketing consulting firm, Jeffrey was vice president, marketing, and a corporate vice president of Loctite Corporation. He was also director of marketing for the wine division of The Pillsbury Co., and held various senior-level marketing jobs at international firms. Jeffrey is the winner of *Sales & Marketing Management* magazine's Outstanding Marketer Award, the American Marketing Association's Outstanding Marketer in Connecticut, and the National Industrial Distributors Award as the Nation's Best Industrial Marketer. He is the subject of a Harvard Business School case study that is rated one of the top 100 case studies, and is thought to be the most widely taught marketing case in the world.

Jeffrey graduated from Trinity College in Hartford, Connecticut, and earned his MBA from Harvard Business School. He served as Trustee of Trinity College, and has won several alumni awards including Person of the Year. He is a member of the Board of Directors of Saint Francis Hospital, one of the nation's top 100 hospitals. He lives in Connecticut.